TOUGH TIMES, STRONG CHILDREN

For Mary,

Dan Kindlon

TOUGH TIMES, STRONG CHILDREN

LESSONS FROM THE PAST FOR YOUR CHILDREN'S FUTURE

DAN KINDLON, PH.D.

miramax books

HYPERION

NEW YORK

Library of Congress Cataloging-in-Publication Data

ISBN: 0-7868-6912-7

FIRST EDITION

10 9 8 7 6 5 4 3 2 1

CONTENTS

———

v

CONTENTS

PART THREE

PREFACE

———

I am a child psychologist. In my spare time I like to read history and as I read, I often find myself wondering about the unseen characters in most history books—the children. How was it for kids to grow up in the shadow of the Civil War, Wounded Knee, or the Black Death? What did widows of wars or the plague do for their children? What did a once proud Sioux warrior tell his children as they grew up on a reservation, dependent on the government? What did these parents do to help their children cope? Were there whole generations of traumatized kids?

In the wake of 9/11, I suddenly found myself, the father of two young children, caught up in a tragic historical event. The world in which my children were growing up had shifted on its axis. The rules had changed. It was no longer clear that they would always enjoy the comfort and security that most of us, I think, had taken for granted. This was a kind of stress that children like mine (and probably yours) had never experienced.

In my two decades of work as a research psychologist, I have often studied the effects of stress on families: conditions such as poverty, exposure to violence, and absent fathers. In my clinical practice I have worked one-on-one or in small groups with children who have had to cope with stressors such as loss of a parent, illness, being bullied, or having a learning disability. But now, faced with stress that felt more global, amorphous, and lethal, I felt unsure about whether what I knew about children, stress, and coping was enough to protect my children. I wanted to be able to do whatever was in my power to immunize my children against stress. So I set out to learn more.

I read all the research I could find on stress and coping, exploring new niches in the field and rereading the classic psychological studies on stress with new eyes—eyes that had seen two jetliners crash into the twin towers.

And I also looked back—to lessons we can learn from the kids who grew up in tough times but survived and even thrived. I felt we needed those lessons, and that our children might need them, too. I interviewed some remarkable people, many of them in their eighties and nineties. I listened to their stories with new ears. Their lives seemed relevant to mine in a way they hadn't before 9/11. Then I started writing this book to put down what I had learned.

PART ONE

CHAPTER 1

The End of Innocence

9/11. The Washington Monument lay on its side. The Capitol building, next to it, was only slightly damaged. The Leaning Tower of Pisa had toppled over and was resting near the Great Pyramid, its base askew. Julia, my eight-year-old daughter, had spent much of the day knocking over these miniature tourist mementos and then standing them up again. If she had owned a miniature version of the World Trade Center's twin towers, it would have been on the floor of her bedroom, too.

"She was so wound up," said my wife, Catalina, when I returned home the next night from Washington, D.C., where I'd been on the morning of the attacks. "It was almost impossible to get her to sleep. She hasn't stopped talking."

Every parent knows the feeling when your child is in distress. You can't stand the thought that she's in pain and you want to make it better.

I looked into Julia's room. She was asleep, her slight frame coiled into a fetal position. The night-light cast a warm reddish glow on her angelic face. When the attacks came, I had been in Washington for an NPR interview, which, needless to say, was canceled.

————

As with many of us, as the news of 9/11 sank in, my concern was for my kids. What kind of world would they grow up in? Would they live in fear and danger? Would their daily life be affected? Would their freedoms be curtailed? Had we given them the tools to cope?

I thought hard about these questions on the drive the next day from Washington to Boston. Finally home, I was relieved to see Julia sleeping peacefully. But the play scenario Catalina described had an eerie familiarity for me. My daughter had created a scene straight from a play therapy textbook.

Over the years I had seen children in my clinical practice create various scenes in order to "work out" or master difficult emotional situations. They had, for example, tried to come to terms with divorce by playing with figures in a dollhouse; in scene after scene, the father packed his suitcase and moved away.

Julia's play was about control. She, not terrorists, had the fate of those buildings in her hands. This sense of mastery helped alleviate her anxiety. It reminded me of the time she had locked herself out of the house. She had been terrified. But soon after this incident she developed a game: She would lock herself in the crawl space under the stairs and then free herself, establishing her control over locked doors.

Across the country many children had, like Julia, tried to come to grips with the terrorist attacks through play. One mother told me of her four-year-old boy who, after his lower Manhattan neighborhood had been turned into a war zone, repeatedly built block towers and then knocked them over with a model plane. Another mother reported that her boy had frequent nightmares after the attacks and drew picture after picture of a plane smashing into the twin towers. These children, like Julia, sought to control these frightening events rather than be controlled by them.

9/11 was the most scared that Julia had ever been. She had been afraid before, of course: A spate of gruesome nightmares had landed her in our bed. She had gone through a phase of thinking there were monsters in her closet. Catalina and I had recently made the mistake of letting her watch *Gone with the Wind.* Julia had become fearful that a modern version of a renegade Union soldier would terrorize our family in the way his movie counterpart had terrorized Scarlett O'Hara.

The fear that 9/11 provoked, however, was of a different caliber. Julia had read the anxiety in her mother's face and the tightness in the voices of her teachers at school. The adults around her told her to not to worry, but they weren't convincing.

Julia was at a tough age as far as fear is concerned. She could perceive danger and imagine its consequences with a sophistication unavailable to a younger child, but she was not old enough to effectively cope with her fears. She felt very vulnerable. Her capacity for denial and rationalization was not fully developed. The invulnerable-teen syndrome—the "it can't happen to me" attitude that drives so many parents crazy—was years away.

Level of fear in children (and adults, for that matter) has to do with both the intensity of the event and one's proximity to it. Proximity has to do with physical distance *and* emotional distance. Television has broken down both our geographical and emotional distance from far-flung events that, literally, come into our living rooms.

Julia had used the miniature buildings to alleviate her anxiety, and they had helped. But I knew that now that I was home and could hold her in my arms she would feel safe again—at least for a little while. For children, the presence of a parent is all-important.

When Julia woke up at dawn on September 13th, we hugged each other for a long time.

Another Place and Time

When I was Julia's age, I had a similar encounter with fear.

I was sitting in the kitchen with my mother, listening to the radio as President Kennedy addressed the nation at the height of the Cuban missile crisis. My mother wore a gray house dress and walked back and forth between the kitchen and dining room, setting the table, finishing dinner preparations. When Kennedy began to speak, she stopped. There was something poised, expectant in her posture. My father wasn't home, probably away on one of his frequent business trips. My mother looked scared, very different from her usual demeanor of someone in control, both of her emotions and the situation. I listened closely to what Kennedy was saying. I didn't understand the politics. But fear rippled through my body each time he mentioned the word "war."

Like many children who grew up during the cold war, I had recurring nightmares about nuclear devastation. In my dreams, I searched through my suburban neighborhood, which had been reduced to rubble, for my parents. Off in the distance, mushroom clouds bloomed in the sky and the earth shook.

These nightmares were reinforced during the day by frequent air raid drills at school. The bell would go off and we'd hustle into the hall, sit against the wall, and put our heads between our knees. The rationale for this rather pointless maneuver was that away from the windows we'd be protected from the blast.

Yet these trials are nothing compared to what many children have had to face, and still do. Kids growing up in Rwanda, Bosnia, Eritrea, Tibet, Colombia, and Northern Ireland have lived with danger that is far more palpable than air raid drills and radio broadcasts.[1] How many children in the world today are refugees as a result of a political upheaval or war? How many have been born into families that have been targets for ethnic cleansing? How many have lived in fear of random violence? How many have never felt safe?

My childhood was relatively stress-free compared to that of many of the kids I see in my clinical practice. I have sat with children who have suffered physical abuse, who are suicidal, whose mother or father has been taken from them by disease, accident, murder, or suicide. I've watched the way these children struggle to comprehend the incomprehensible.

I have watched them lose their innocence as they realize that life isn't fair, that bad things can happen to good children, and that a parent's assurance that the world is a safe place is false. Human nature and human relationships are complex. Evil exists. Some kids are confronted with these realizations early. A kid in inner-city Chicago grows up faster than Julia, who goes to school in Wellesley, a sheltered haven, cloistered from much of the sadness, evil, and suffering that plagues the wider world.

It's important for us as parents to understand the process our children go through as they cross the border between warm childhood innocence and cold reality. How, as parents, can we prepare them for that journey if we don't have a map?

For some children, depending on their life circumstances and temperament, the crossing may be gradual, a natural part of life; for others it is a stark, traumatic change. Most children eventually learn to cope with unfairness, grief, and fear. Others don't. Some become addicted to self-pity or lash out against the world. Others numb themselves with alcohol and drugs. Still others never become fully functional. They have deep fears lodged inside them, which inhibit them and keep them from giving fully of themselves.

The Millennials and Resilience

Growing up in the unprecedented prosperity and domestic tranquillity of the 1980s and 1990s, our children, by and large, have been sheltered from much of the hardships of life, and the stress that goes along with it. 9/11 and the new world order that has followed are a wake-up call for us as parents. We now know we need to help our children face the difficulties that are an inevitable part of life with courage and resilience.

Resilience, like many psychological terms, has its roots in physics. Resilient substances are those that can absorb a shock or stress and bounce back to their original shape and form. In human terms, this means that a child is resilient who falls off her bike, scrapes her knee, dusts herself off, and climbs back on for another try. It means a child who is able to take criticism and not buckle. It means a child who is able to persist and not give up when faced with difficulties, whether it's a subject she's trying to master, a musical instrument, or a friendship that is on the rocks.

The psychological study of resilience is relatively new. I remember as a freshly minted Ph.D. in 1981 hearing Norman Garmezy—the father of resilience research—address the International Congress of Child Psychiatry in Dublin.[2] He urged us to study not just the suffering and the sick, and the severe life-pressure that can lead to mental illness and behavior problems. He also urged us to study the psychology of ordinary people who survived and even thrived in the face of adversity.

Garmezy was interested in the experiences of disadvantaged inner-city children, not just those kids who had succumbed to adverse family circumstances (broken homes or abusive parents) and high-crime neighborhoods, but also kids who had faced difficulties and bounced back. He was convinced that social scientists could learn as much, if not more, from studying health as we could from studying pathology.

The psychological research that has focused on resilient children has taught us much. We have learned that a child's genetic endowment can predispose him toward resilience. We have also learned that factors outside the child's control—his attractiveness to others, and the quality of his family, neighborhood, and peer group, for example—are important for coping with stress and adversity. Moreover, we have learned that any child's resilience can be enhanced by skills, attitudes, and abilities taught to them by committed, loving adults. Our loving attention is the foundation on which to build a child's resistance to stress and help them cope with adversity. Once learned, these tools can help protect our children and make them resilient.

––––––––

In the days after 9/11, as I struggled to come to terms with what the attacks meant for our children, I grew increasingly concerned that the current generation of kids is ill equipped to deal with hard times. For the Millennials (the generation whose oldest members are coming of age at the dawn of the millennium) this has meant unprecedented expectations of material comfort, good health, success, prestige, and satisfaction in the workplace. Of course, we all want these things for our kids, but when unrealistically high expectations go unmet, they often lead to disappointment and stress.

Today's kids have little sense of perspective about the level of comfort in their lives. They don't understand, for example, that they are lucky simply to be alive, that childhood diseases—tuberculosis, rheumatic fever, polio, pneumonia, and meningitis—have nearly disappeared in the

Western world. Yet among children aged five to fourteen, the rate of reported illness rose 233 percent between 1928 and 1981. Our kids think they're sick when they have complaints that earlier generations would have dismissed as trivial.[3] Their sense of entitlement to good health, to ease and comfort, make me worry that they are unprepared to meet challenges in the future.

I recently met a woman who works as a production manager on films when they shoot scenes on location—a process that usually takes a month or two to complete.

As part of her job, she had to hire people, many of whom were in their early twenties. She said that for the first time in her experience many of these young people come to her during production and want to quit because the job doesn't meet their expectations. "They want it to be more fulfilling and not such hard work," she told me. "That never happened ten years ago. Everybody used to be able to stick it out for the whole six weeks."

We don't want our children to "settle" for a job that doesn't fulfill them, shun treatment for physical pain or illness, or unnecessarily deny themselves comfort or pleasure. But some hardship, failure, and suffering will help them appreciate what is good in their lives. We want to know that, if necessary, they can meet adversity, test their limits, make sacrifices, and develop effective coping responses. My clinical sense, however, suggests that most of them are too self-centered, too sheltered, to do this. Their self-centeredness is magnified by and contributes to an erosion of social cohesion, a weakening of our connections to one another. When our communities are fragile, we lose strength, we lose resilience, and we compromise our survival in the face of adversity.

The Millennials were born into an America that President Jimmy Carter, when he was in office, said was beset by a malaise—a crisis of spirit characterized by "the worship of self-indulgence and consumption."[4] Shortly after Carter diagnosed us, Madonna released a hit CD (*Like a Virgin*, 1984) that opened with "Material Girl." The song's lyrics unabashedly celebrate materialism:

> We are living in a material world
> And I am a material girl

I am not denying the importance of money, merely pointing out its deification in many segments of our society. This "It's all about the Benjamins" philosophy (hundred-dollar bills, for those of you unfamiliar with the Puff Daddy song) permeates the atmosphere our children breathe as they grow up. They can't help but be affected by it.

Today's incoming college freshmen say that "becoming very well off financially" is their number-one objective for attending college. The proportion of freshmen that consider this "very important" or "essential" has risen from 39 percent in 1970 to 74 percent in 1998. In 1970, the year when many of their parents were college-aged, the most important reason stated for going to college was to "develop a meaningful philosophy of life."[5]

Too often, the focus on the material world results in self-centeredness. Two generations ago, the ultra-wealthy John D. Rockefeller was fond of the Biblical quote[6]: "For unto whomsoever much is given, of him shall be much required." [Luke 12:48] He followed these words by creating the philanthropic Rockefeller Foundation. A generation ago, John F. Kennedy sounded a similar note, "Our privileges can be no greater than our obligations," he said.[7] Today, the values that accompany affluence are summed up in the advertising slogan: Indulge yourself.

In the 1990s, Americans donated a smaller share of their personal income to charitable causes than at any time since the 1940s. Philanthropy's share of Americans' income fell from 2.26 percent of income in 1964 to 1.61 percent in 1998, a relative decline of 29 percent. In 1960 we gave away about one dollar for every two dollars we spent on recreation; in 1997, we gave less than fifty cents.[8]

These self-centered values, as I'll discuss in subsequent chapters, can make it more difficult for children to cope with adversity. Moreover, a "me-first" attitude can compromise the health of our society when a crisis demands personal sacrifice.

Aside from expectations, other factors influence our kids' ability to deal with stress. In Part Two, we'll discuss the following points in depth. But I think they're worth noting, briefly, here.

Declining Religious Participation

Imagine the inside of your favorite bookstore. You probably see shelves of fiction, hundreds and hundreds of books subdivided into Mystery, Science Fiction, Romance, Classics, New Releases, Best-sellers, books about sports, cookbooks, scores of diet books. Parenting and Childcare have their own section. The History section, where I spend a lot of my time, may have a whole case devoted to books on the American Civil War or the works of Steven Ambrose.

Psychology and self-help books are also popular. The section on religious books is often quite small compared to the store's other sections.

A century ago, however, the Religion section would have occupied most of the store. Before 1900 there were more religious publications printed in a year than all other books combined![9]

This tremendous change reflects the rise of secularism. Not long ago the Bible would have been one of the only books found in a home. It would have been revered and constantly referred to as a source of wisdom and guidance, and it would have been read daily.[10]

Many Millennial children are growing up without the security that religion can provide. Whatever else can be said of religion, it can be useful when it comes to coping with stress. A popular saying in World War II was "There are no atheists in foxholes." Many of the people you will meet in Part Two of this book said that it was their religious faith— often transmitted to them through their parents—which enabled them to recover from the hardships they faced.

Community

Along with religion, a sense of community can be vitally important when it comes to facing adversity. I interviewed the wife of a navy doctor, now in her eighties, who had to move from Chicago to Norfolk, Virginia, with her two-year-old twins at the start of World War II. She endured long separations from her husband when he was shipped out. She credits the community of navy wives, women with whom she has remained in touch for over fifty years, for making the experience bearable. "When we were in Norfolk, Virginia, we were so close," she said. "It was just like family. You didn't feel alone. When you first got out there you thought you were stranded. But before too long you got to meet the other families. We could always tap in on one another and be there for one another. That was what helped all of us survive the war."

Sadly, our sense of community, our sense of belonging to a larger group, has eroded over the past two decades. Harvard professor Robert Putnam says that suburban sprawl, television, the Internet, and time pressure have contributed to this breakdown. We attend fewer civic meetings, and form fewer bowling leagues or other community groups. The once common practice of hitchhiking has almost disappeared from the American landscape. Our sense of trust and connection with our fellow man has diminished.[11]

Time and the Lack Thereof

The building blocks of communities are families. Sociologists today debate the precise definition of the "family unit." Is a family everyone who lives under one roof, people with a strong genetic link, or some larger constellation of people? The definition of family that I prefer: Family is where you go when no one else will take you—a place of refuge in hard times.

Family is usually the most important support a child has.

This is one of the reasons that divorce tends to be so hard on children—their fundamental sense of safety is threatened.

The widely reported demise of the American family is not due solely to the increase in divorce and single parenting. As important is the decline in family time (even in two-parent families) that has occurred during the past two decades. Household conversation, just sitting and talking, has declined by 100 percent over this period. The time that children used to spend with family is now spent on sports and homework. Sports participation by children has doubled since 1981; and time spent in school and studying time have also increased. Some of these changes are tied to the fact that women have entered the workforce in large numbers. In 1950, 12 percent of moms worked, in 1980, 47 percent; in 1997, 67 percent.[12]

The support kids need when they're faced with difficulties is, first and foremost, our presence. The half-awake hug Julia gave me on September 13th expresses every child's needs.

Conclusion

When times are good, many of us don't need the support of community, religion, family, or friends. We aren't required to make personal sacrifices for the common good. But as 9/11 reminded us, we are all dependent on one another and interconnected. We are bound together by a social contract. We need the support of our family, neighbors, community, and friends.

In my last book, *Too Much of a Good Thing*, I compared

Millennials to the generation that came of age at the turn of the twentieth century and became known as the Lost Generation—a generation often characterized by aimlessness and hedonism. Then I contrasted them with the Greatest Generation—men and women hardened during the Great Depression who rose to the challenges and sacrifices of WWII.[13] The character of the Millennial Generation—especially for its younger members—has not yet solidified. The plaster is still wet and we—parents, teachers, and mentors—are its sculptors.

The more we understand about how children cope with adversity, the better able we'll be to help our kids face the challenges of an uncertain future. With that in mind, let's take a look at the biology and psychology of stress and how it typically affects children.

CHAPTER 2

Children, Stress, and Coping

8/24/92: In what was arguably the worst natural disaster in U.S. history, the winds of Hurricane Andrew howled across South Florida's Dade County at 164 miles per hour. Children watched as windows shattered and roofs blew off. Scores of people died.

Andrew's aftermath prolonged the devastation. The relief effort was poorly coordinated. Looting was prevalent. Millions were without water and power. Many people lost their jobs when businesses closed. By October, more than 10,000 school children—25 percent of Dade County's school population—had fled the area with their families.

I remember watching the televised scenes of children leaving the wreckage that had once been home. They carried toys, perhaps a favorite doll or teddy bear. I knew these children also carried away something else—frightening, vivid memories that would affect them long after Andrew's winds had died.

Follow-up research on the children and adolescents who lived in the hurricane's path showed that most of these children's fears gradually subsided. The frequency of their nightmares decreased, and they were once again able to concentrate on their schoolwork. They began to have hope for the future. A minority, however (5 to 10 percent), had psychological wounds that did not heal.[1]

———

Social scientists wanted to learn why some children did better with the stress of Andrew than others. Their studies of Andrew's victims were informed by an event that occurred six and a half years earlier.

On January, 18, 1986, the American space shuttle *Challenger* was launched and television networks had scheduled a special broadcast across the country. Children in Concord, New Hampshire, gathered in their classroom just before lunch, watched with particular interest because Christa McAuliffe, a local high school teacher, was aboard.

Blast off! Seventy-three seconds later the shuttle exploded. Students stared at the screen, too shocked to react. Then, some started crying. On the West Coast, children were not yet in school, but nearly all would soon hear about the disaster and watch graphic photos and televised replays of the event.

Child psychologists and psychiatrists were called into Concord and elsewhere to help children cope with the psychological aftermath of the explosion. Researchers (psychologists mostly) came into the schools, too, studying the effects of second-hand trauma on children. One study compared children's reactions in Concord to those in Pottersville, California,[2] where the children had no close emotional connection to McAuliffe and they had not seen the event live.

Six weeks after the disaster nearly all the children in Concord, especially those in grade school, had stress-related psychological or physical symptoms. They relived the disaster in writing, drawing or the kind of repetitive reenactment in which my daughter Julia had engaged after the World Trade Center attack. Some were afraid to fly; some became morbid; some were "clingy," afraid to be alone. A few had chronic stomachaches.

In California, a smaller percentage of children appeared affected by the event. Still, the majority were symptomatic—which is remarkable, given their distance from the event. As with Hurricane Andrew, a year later most of these symptoms had disappeared, both in Concord and California. For some children, however, the disaster lived on in their dreams, fears, and outlook for the future. These children would carry the burden of the trauma with them into later life.

———

Traumatizing events can be acute or ongoing (chronic). Both the *Challenger* disaster and Hurricane Andrew were acute events. The *Challenger* was gone in an instant; Andrew's life-threatening winds died down in a matter of hours. Research showed that short-lived though they were, Andrew and the shuttle disaster profoundly affected the children who experienced them.

Examples of long-term stress include the challenges of living with a chronic illness—cancer or diabetes—or living in constant fear of physical or sexual abuse. Some children grow up in violent neighborhoods. In war-torn Liberia, Chechnya, and East Timor entire generations of children have never known peace.[3] Yet, even under the weight of chronic stress, many of these kids will grow into fully functional adults.

Differing reactions to stress are one of the most perplexing riddles of human psychology. Behavioral scientists have started to systematically study stress and coping only within the last thirty years. Stress research that focuses exclusively on children has been conducted during an even shorter period. Although the field is still in its infancy and there is much that we don't know, there has been some progress.[4] The science of stress and recovery is beginning to yield results that can help parents immunize their children against the harmful effects of stress.

Stress and Trauma

The words *stress* and *trauma* are used to refer to different circumstances and conditions. Stress is the more general term, having its origin in physics, referring to the weight or load on a structure such as a bridge (this is why we say we feel "weighed down" by stress). The cause of stress (sometimes referred to as a *stressor*) can be mild—carrying the psychological weight of a car going over the Golden Gate Bridge—or it can be severe. Its strain can tax our capacity to bear up under it. Unfortunately for research scientists, psychological stressors cannot be accurately weighed. What one person experiences as heavy stress is barely noticed by another. Any parent or teacher knows, for example, that some children are more stressed out being in a school play than others, and that these same stage-frightened children may be the *least* afraid of the kids in the class when it comes to handling spiders and snakes in science demonstrations.

Stress is also a *feeling* accompanied by physiological changes. Anxiety, dread, a pounding heart, and sweaty palms are common symptoms of stress. The character of these feelings and the biology of stress will be discussed in detail a bit later in this chapter.

The word *trauma*, like *stress*, is used to refer to both something external—a traumatic event—as well as our reaction to it (the state of being traumatized). Traumatic events are out-of-the-ordinary and severe: natural disasters, abuse, combat, and rape, for example. The severity of such events, and most importantly the fact that one usually feels helpless in the face of them, makes them qualitatively different from mere stress. It's not only the event itself but a person's reaction that causes psychologists to classify it as traumatic. In a somewhat circular definition, an event is deemed traumatic (rather than merely extremely stressful) if one becomes traumatized by it—that is, develops the symptoms of post-traumatic stress disorder (PTSD). More about what those symptoms are later.

Everyone has experienced stress. Most of us—over three fourths of American adults—have experienced extreme stress. PTSD is comparatively rare: estimates are that 8 percent of American adults and 5 percent of teenagers have had PTSD.[5]

Stress on the Inside

Our biological responses to stress are largely under the control of some of our more primitive brain structures, the limbic system—parts of our brain that are similar in structure and function to the brains of "lower" mammals. These brain structures and the stress responses they generate evolved to adapt to the threats to survival inherent in the animal world.

Human society has, of course, been evolving faster than these old brain structures, which means that the physiological changes that occur in response to social stress, such as public speaking or being introduced to a roomful of strangers, are pretty much the same as those that happen to a baboon when he senses that he is being stalked by a leopard.

Our ancestors (both human and animal) faced stress that was short-term and intense. A gibbon stalked by a leopard would experience intense stress, but usually only for a short time. The gibbon was either eaten, or the leopard moved on to easier prey.

For ancient man, too, the stress he faced was generally short-lived and intense. Today, however, many of us live with constant stress, partially because we can imagine the future, and partially because the threats to our welfare, while they may not be as acute as a hungry leopard or Hurricane Andrew, can lurk, insidiously, in the background of our lives. We worry about illness, finance, or romance.

This discrepancy between our "primitive" stress response system and the realities of our modern world—where we are chronically on high alert—causes both physical and mental problems for us. It has also, for better or worse, created the need for psychologists.

23

There are two primary types of biological response to stress. The first occurs instantaneously whenever we perceive a threatening situation. Imagine that you are driving in the car with your children late at night. It is drizzling. The road is dark. Suddenly, out of nowhere, a deer runs in front of your car. You swerve to avoid a potentially deadly crash.

The rapid bodily changes that occur in reaction to the stress of almost hitting the deer are a physiological call to battle that mobilizes your body for action (flight or fight). In brief, what happens is that your sympathetic nervous system, which connects your brain to your body's organs, glands, and blood vessels, is activated, and the neurotransmitters epinephrine and norepinephrine are released into your system (in Britain these are called *adrenaline* and *noradrenaline*).

The action of these neurotransmitters is like an injection of strong coffee directly into our brains. We become instantly alert. Our pupils dilate. Our heart rate increases, and energy-giving blood rushes into the muscles of the arms and legs, preparing us to run or fight. At the same time, energy is diverted from all nonessential functions; the sympathetic nervous system inhibits digestive processes, sexual arousal, the immune system, and growth functions.

The second type of biological response to stress is a little slower getting under way. It is responsible for maintaining the flight-or-fight response for as long as the stress lasts and also helps to turn off the stress response when the danger has passed.

This slower response, which kicks in about fifteen seconds after the stress is perceived, starts in an old part of the brain called the hypothalamus. Once the hypothalamus gets the "red-alert" signal from the brain centers responsible for evaluating stress, it secretes hormones that tell another old brain structure—the pituitary—to send out other hormones that tell various bodily organs, including the adrenal glands, what to do.

Sugar is released into the blood so that energy becomes available to the muscles. Endorphins, which dull pain, are also released. Nonnecessary functions, such as those involved in reproduction, growth, and fighting viruses, are further inhibited from the first-phase stress responses. We are focused on the emergency at hand—everything else recedes. Any mother who has had to take an injured child to the emergency room or lost her child in a store knows what this feeling is like.

Shutting down the immune system, growth functions, and other nonessential bodily activities isn't harmful for short periods. Stress response over a longer period, however, can cause chronic high blood pressure, ulcers, growth retardation, depression, and lowered resistance to infection.[6]

It is this last symptom that prompted much of the early interest in stress. A classic study on the relationship between stress and illness was conducted by Sheldon Cohen at Carnegie Mellon University and published in the prestigious *New England Journal of Medicine* in 1991.[7]

Cohen, in collaboration with scientists in the U.K., exposed healthy adults to a cold virus by dripping a salt water solution containing a low infectious dose (approximately equivalent with what you would get if you came in close contact with someone who had a contagious cold) of the virus into their nose. These people were quarantined for two days before they were exposed and seven days after exposure.

After seven days, 82 percent of the people exposed to the virus showed signs of infection (biological indicators of virus-specific antibodies) and 38 percent had noticeable cold symptoms. The most interesting finding of the study was that the more stressed a person was before they were exposed to the cold virus (based on questionnaires administered at the beginning of the study), the more likely he or she was to be infected or have a cold. This was true even when these scientists were careful to control other factors such as age, gender, and whether the person smoked or exercised regularly.

The overall wear and tear on the body that results from chronic stress is termed *allostatic load*.[8] When researchers study people who have experienced high levels of chronic stress, such as concentration camp survivors or combat veterans, they find that stress hormones can, over time, cause irreparable harm, including brain damage and memory impairment.[9]

Gender Bias?

Shelley Taylor and her colleagues at the University of California have recently proposed that the flight-or-fight stress response is more of a male pattern—promulgated by men doing research on male rats—and that female stress response is marked more by a "tend-and-befriend" pattern.[10]

Taylor has advanced the idea that women are more likely to nurture offspring and seek companionship—the protection of a group—when under stress, a pattern that emerged during evolution because of the demands on women of pregnancy, nursing, and caring for children.

These scientists further propose that this tend-and-befriend pattern may be influenced a different set of hormones and neurotransmitters (female ones) than flight-or-fight.

These intriguing findings may, one day, be incorporated into the psychological canon, but they do not alter the basic biological facts I have just presented. Taylor freely admits that the biological core of stress responses is roughly equivalent for men and women. Moreover, chronic stress is deleterious—it brings illness, depression, and eventually neurological damage—to both sexes.

Manifestations of Stress and Trauma in Children and Adolescents

Part of our reaction to stress is emotional—we feel anxious, upset, worried, fearful, agitated, paralyzed, angry. Children and adolescents often act out these feelings (adults do, too, of course). That is, the feelings translate into behavior. Unfortunately for the science of psychology, these behavioral responses to stress are not clear-cut. Children and adolescents manifest stress in a myriad of ways.

A common response to stress in kids is the repetitive play exhibited by my daughter, Julia. In repetitive play, people who are "killed" can be brought back to life; buildings resurrected from rubble. Repetitive play comes, in part, from a desire to control largely uncontrollable events.

27

Regression—a sudden reversion to immature patterns of behavior—is another common response to stress in children. A toilet-trained child will start soiling himself. Children may revert to immature speech or start sucking their thumbs. They may become clingy and dependent, wanting us close by at bedtime, afraid to play alone. They may have difficulty getting to sleep or they may have nightmares—a common response to stress.

Regression appears during times of stress because our children don't have the psychological energy to function at a mature level (similar to an adult who is whiny or short tempered when tired). A regressed child returns to a time when he was more dependent—when he could feel safe hiding beneath parental wings.

Illness is another common symptom of stress. A stressed child is more likely to get sick. Physical symptoms, such as headaches, stomachaches, and muscular or joint pain (real or imagined) often occur. Stomachaches are quite common—anxiety tends to affect the digestive system. Like regression, illness, real or perceived, can serve to keep our children close; their symptoms may require our vigilance and attention. They may have to stay home from school. In many cases, a sick child will recover almost as soon as the cause of the stress disappears.

Our children may also become aggressive when they're stressed. Two children from the same family may experience the same stressor, such as divorce. Both may be equally upset, but one may withdraw quietly, shunning contact, while the other becomes hostile, angry, and destructive. Many children manifest sadness and depression as irritability. For others, irritability escalates to anger.[11]

Post-Traumatic Stress Disorder

If a child experiences extreme stress—an earthquake, rape, or assault—he may manifest symptoms of post-traumatic stress disorder (PTSD).

There are generally three classes of PTSD symptoms. First, the traumatic event may be persistently reexperienced in vivid, disturbing dreams or memories, repetitive play, or "flashbacks." During flashbacks, a child thinks the traumatic event is actually recurring.

The reexperiencing of stress, however, need not take the form of the event that produced the stress. Children's nightmares do not necessarily contain explicit content from an actual trauma. Similarly, repetitive play may be semirealistic or even symbolic.

A second class of post-traumatic symptoms involves avoiding situations or persons associated with the traumatic event. A child may consciously have an I-don't-want-to-talk-about-it attitude, or he can have post-traumatic amnesia, in which details of the traumatic event can't be recalled. Avoidance often takes the form of psychic numbing. The child may appear unfeeling, detached from others.

A third class of PTSD symptoms includes difficulty concentrating, sleeplessness, edginess, and severe irritability.[12]

———————

I've had first-hand experience with PTSD symptoms. Fifteen years ago my wife and I were at our obstetrician's for our final prenatal visit. This was our first child. The visit took place a few days prior to the baby's due date, and we expected labor to begin at any moment.

The doctor attached the heart rate monitor to my wife's swollen abdomen. He didn't immediately hear the heartbeat, and we laughed when he made a lighthearted comment about the baby making things difficult for him. But then his expression changed. He was no longer smiling. We could feel his tension. He told us to rush to the delivery room. We ran to the car and drove five minutes to Boston's Brigham and Women's Hospital. We were frantic in the elevator because we couldn't remember the floor for obstetrics. Well-meaning people laughed and told us not to worry, that we had plenty of time. As it turned out, they were right. Our baby was already dead. What followed was a nightmarish three days in which we stayed in the hospital and tried to deliver the baby.

After we finally delivered our stillborn child, we went home and dismantled the nursery. My wife no longer needed maternity leave and went back to work, as did I. My office at the Harvard Medical School was not far from Brigham and Women's Hospital. I made a habit of avoiding "The Brigham," as it is known locally, which was usually possible without going too far out of my way.

But one day, several months after the fateful prenatal visit, I drove by the hospital, forgetting to take my normal circuitous route. My path was identical to the one my wife and I had taken on our frantic trip to the obstetrics unit. Suddenly, my perception of the scene changed; I was transported back in time to that horrifying day. It is difficult to describe the feeling except to say that I was there again. The flashback lasted only fifteen seconds. I have never had another, at least with that intensity of feeling. I have been to the hospital many times since. My two living daughters were born there. Whenever I'm there, I feel sad; but the memories are nowhere near as vivid or intense as my flashback. That flashback has given me an understanding of what traumatized people go through—the power of the experience, its unpredictability, and our helplessness in the face of it.

Absence of Symptoms

Some of the findings on children and stress seem counterintuitive—there are children whom we would expect to show manifestations of stress who don't. Research on children with chronic illness is a case in point. Approximately 6 percent of all American children under the age of twenty suffer from chronic illnesses, including asthma, cerebral palsy, diabetes mellitus, paralysis, congenital heart disease, and seizure disorders.

These children often have their education disrupted. Their physical and social activities may be limited or curtailed. They may have to undergo periodic painful medical procedures and live in uncertainty about their future health or survival. Yet despite all this, children with chronic illness are no more likely than "normal" children to be depressed, have low self-esteem, or show other signs of emotional maladjustment.[13]

It's interesting, as we'll see in later chapters, that some children seem to derive some benefit from stress. Laurel

Holliday, who has interviewed scores of children who have grown up amid the violence between Catholics and Protestants in Northern Ireland, writes: "In keeping with what I have long suspected about children who grow up challenged by war, poverty, parental loss—even 'dysfunctional families' as we Americans rather mechanically call them—I found no empirical support for the idea that they will necessarily have lifelong psychological problems. Although there are people who have suffered serious consequences of many kinds of trauma in Northern Ireland, I believe that sometimes such serious challenges precipitate greater flexibility and maturity than a placid life of plenty. Sometimes truly compassionate and wise adults are born of painful, even torturous childhoods."[14]

Many factors affect whether a child will emerge from adversity with greater strength of character. Listening to the life stories of some of the remarkable people you will meet in the second section of this book brought this home to me. One such person I had the privilege of interviewing was George McGovern, the former U.S. senator and presidential candidate who is currently working to end world hunger as head of the United Nations Food and Agriculture Organization in Rome.

McGovern, who is eighty years old, is no stranger to stress. He grew up during the Depression, faced death repeatedly as a bomber pilot in World War II, suffered a crushing defeat to Richard Nixon as the Democratic presidential nominee in 1972, and, most significantly, endured pain and heartbreak when his daughter, Terry, lost her battle with alcoholism and froze to death in a snow bank in 1994.

Despite these hardships, McGovern remains undefeated, a loving father and grandfather, an optimistic believer in the power of human kindness. At an age when many of his contemporaries spend their time enjoying a well-deserved rest on the golf course, he continues to do significant community service.

"I have never understood people who dwell on their problems," he told me. "I've never been that way. I'm not saying that I didn't have some difficult times. But I didn't let them take over my life."

You may think that this sounds like a man who is burying his head in the sand to avoid his true feelings, more like pathological denial than successful coping. Aren't psychotherapists always telling people to get in touch with their feelings? Isn't this a lot of what psychological health is all about? In my opinion, psychological health, and, by implication, successful coping, involves a balance between an in-depth understanding of your feelings and the ability to move on, to not let those feelings dominate our lives.

It is impossible to talk with McGovern for more than a few minutes and still believe that he is hiding his true feelings. He talked to me about how the sorrow of losing his daughter was almost unbearable, that it was sadder than anything he could have imagined.[15] But McGovern faced his feelings and came to terms with his anger, sadness, and guilt. He went on to live his life.

McGovern's successful coping may have been due, in part, to a sturdy constitution—a biological advantage. Some of the factors involved in successful coping are biological, as we will see in the next section of this chapter, and are largely beyond a parent's control. But we will also see in Part Two of this book how McGovern's parents—as all parents can—helped immunize him against the stress that he later encountered.

Temperament

Our overweight indoor cats are named Fluffy and King Tut. Fluffy is dark gray with muted stripes. Tut, the larger of the pair, has an orange coat the color of sherbet and a white patch on his throat that hangs like a pendant. Both are affectionate animals, happy to curl up on your lap, loudly purring as you try to read.

Temperamentally, however, they are as different as night and day. The doorbell rings. It's FedEx or a neighbor. Tut scampers to the door, ready to bolt when it opens, pining for the great outdoors where he can hide in the bushes, stalking real and imaginary prey.

Fluffy, on the other hand, takes off as soon she hears the bell. If she is the front hallway, her feet spin on the floor as she tries to get traction. When she gets her footing, she shoots up the stairs and runs into the attic through the hinged cat door.

Cat breeders and animal researchers know that there are two groups of cats: a minority like Fluffy, skittish and fearful; the majority more like Tut, adventurous, bold, unafraid of new people and most novel situations.

Animal studies indicate that there are neurological differences between these two types. The basal amygdala (part of the brain's limbic system) in a fearful cat's brain is more reactive, more sensitive to cues of danger, more excitable than the basal amygdala of its adventurous counterpart. It takes less to stimulate the flight-or-fight response in cats like Fluffy.[16]

Is there a human parallel? Yes and no. Humans are obviously much more complex than cats—so feline differences are easier to spot. Nevertheless, children do seem to be born with innate differences in temperament.

The scientific study of human temperament is young, and there's still much we don't understand. Much of my academic research has explored temperamental variation in children. It is extremely difficult to know exactly what temperamental dispositions exist, how they are manifest, and how much they are affected by different parenting styles. Research—much of it done by Jerome Kagan at Harvard—indicates that there are a minority of human children, maybe 10 percent, who are a lot like Fluffy. These kids are sometimes characterized as shy, behaviorally inhibited, or timid.

If you tossed a lit firecracker into the back of a quiet classroom, behaviorally inhibited children's heart rates skyrocket when it goes off. They jump from their seats and take longer to calm down after the explosion. An inhibited toddler is more likely to avoid contact with strangers and hide behind his parents.

Timid kids have a counterpart at the other end of the spectrum—kids who are extremely outgoing, largely unafraid, and less neurologically excitable. These temperamental extremes were clear to me when as a young investigator I did a study of eighteen-month-olds. I videotaped them as they entered a strange room with their mother. There were unfamiliar toys in the room. One, in particular, proved useful to my research. It was a mechanical robot that moved around in a low box at the back of the room with lights flashing, motor whirring, and smoke coming from its head.

When they saw the robot, some children would clutch their mother with one hand and keep the other on the door. A pleading look on their faces seemed to say, "Get me outta here!" Other kids reacted in exactly the opposite way. Heedless of danger, they would immediately jump into the box and play with the robot. Most children's behavior fell in between these two extremes.

Being at either end of this spectrum may have implications for coping with stress. A timid child is likely to experience a situation as more stressful than other children. He will have a slower recovery time than other children, and he may develop indelible memories that will cause his fear to generalize, triggering the flight-or-fight response in situations similar to the one that first produced stress. The uninhibited child may find it easier to cope with stressful situations. His experience of stress may be less intense, and he may carry a less powerful memory of the experience into new situations.

————

These behavioral predispositions are inherited, but not as a single dominant or recessive gene; instead, temperament is influenced by many genes. However, biology is not destiny. A propensity towards shyness, for example, may be modified. Kagan found, for example, that an infant born with physiologically reactive tendencies and fearfulness, who is in a supportive environment and experiences no major stress early in life, can undergo changes in those brain circuits that mediate emotional reactivity, and, consequently, when she is older, not show the high reactivity she was born with. There is hope for our children who seem temperamentally prone to fearfulness. Whatever a child's biological predisposition, a parent can help him cope by giving him a sense of control over a situation that produces stress, rather than being a passive victim.

Age Differences in Stress and Coping

Children's reactions to just about anything—food, clothes, sports, school, other kids—change with age. That is one of the most difficult, and often unforeseen, challenges of parenting. Just about the time you figure out how to deal with your child, he gets older, the rules change and you find yourself once again at the bottom of a learning curve. A parent who anticipates these changes is ahead of the game; the learning process doesn't take as long.

Children's responses to stress change with age as do their coping abilities. What follows is a brief overview of some of the age differences a parent might expect.[17]

0–5

Infants under six months tend not to remember distressing experiences, such as painful medical procedures. As such, these children and even children to the age of four or five have a built-in protection against stress not found in older children. But in other ways these children are *more* vulnerable to stress than older children.

In children up to five years old, separation from parents is the most traumatic aspect of stress that they experience. Children often do remarkably well in a stressful situation (little initial fear and few post-stress symptoms) if they are with their parents. Knowing this, children's hospitals now routinely allow parents to stay overnight with their children.

Children under five are generally not capable of reasoning. Thus, parents' attempts to explain the WTC bombings or other catastrophic events at anything approaching an adult level are usually misguided and may cause more stress than they alleviate. As a general rule, if a young child is curious about a stressful or traumatic event, only answer what the child is asking about. A young child's questions about these events will usually focus on his safety (and, possibly, yours). Answer their specific question. Don't explain geopolitics. If they ask, for example, who was responsible for a crime or attack, simply say that they are bad people, but the police (army, president) will do their best to find them and put them in jail. If they ask more questions, answer them, but keep it simple, and remain calm and reassuring.

Tangible reassurance—hugs, a parent's presence, the sense that the world is still predictable and safe—can be very comforting to a child. For toddlers (and all children to some extent) disruption of their routine is stressful. Children have come to expect regularity in their lives and a parent can alleviate much stress by sticking to the child's regular routine as much as possible. If possible, don't disrupt the child's naptime, bedtime, and meals. Keep the child on a regular school, daycare, or childcare schedule. Send the message that the world hasn't fallen apart—signal through your actions that life will go on much as it has in the past.

6–12

Older children are less vulnerable to parental absence—they willingly go to school, sleepovers and overnight camps. There is a big change in cognitive ability (termed *the 5–7 shift* by developmentalists, referring to the age at which it normally occurs). Children can "hold on" to a concept or image in their heads in ways younger children can't. As such, an eight-year-old can think about a parent when he or she is not physically present and be comforted.

A leap in reasoning ability by age eight makes kids sometimes sound like little adults. Many parents make the mistake of assuming that their child's level of emotional intelligence and coping skills are on a par with this new cognitive sophistication. They are not. Children at this age who are exposed to frightening or stressful events are often overwhelmed by strong emotions. Their increased cognitive ability has, in some ways made them more vulnerable to stress.

I think this is one reason that my daughter Julia, who was eight at the time of the WTC attacks, was more frightened than my daughter Diana, who was twelve. As children get older they become more sophisticated at adopting illusions and rationalizations that act as a buffer against fear, sadness and other negative emotions. The capacity for denial, aided in part by brain maturation, also increases with age.[18]

There is a good deal of psychological research that concludes that there are many situations in which a little denial (and this holds true for adults as well as children) may be healthy. By denial I mean, ignoring the facts, distorting reality, refusing to see what's right before our eyes. In some cases, an accurate view of reality may actually contribute to poorer mental health. Thus, the elementary school–aged child will continue to need shielding. She will need her parents to be less than honest in some situations, to act as if things are better than they are, and to be protected from disturbing events. There is a good reason for PG-13 movie ratings.

Teenagers

Three of the main developmental milestones of adolescence are a leap in cognitive sophistication; improved psychological defenses, such as the capacity for denial; and an increase in egocentricity.

Teens begin to be able to think abstractly and envision the future more clearly. They can understand cause and effect better than they did when they were younger. As such, talking about their feelings and what to do about them (when they'll listen) is more effective now than at earlier ages.

Just as cognitive ability takes another big leap during the teenage years, so does coping. In fact one hallmark of adolescence seems to be the ability to deny the existence of reality even when it is staring you in the face. While this can be maddening for a parent trying to explain some of the hazards of having sex "before you're ready," it can also cushion their teen's response to stress.

This well-tuned denial mechanism is balanced and sometimes overwhelmed by increased egocentricity (I never said teenagers weren't confusing). Thus, a teenager may feel that the spotlight is always on him—he gets a zit on the end of his nose and he feels everyone is looking at it. Moreover, he can display an "it's all about me" attitude that defies comprehension. He's upset after the 9/11 attacks because the malls close. If there is a stressful event, he may overdramatize its importance to him personally. He can easily ignore statistical reality and believe that he is the most likely victim of the next attack. Thus, it may be useful for parents of teens to help them decrease their self-consciousness and, with it, their stress. We need to inject humor into their conniptions, asking them (without goading or bullying) to get a grip. We need to remind them that they are not the center of universe, that other people have needs, too, and provide them with factual information that challenges any delusions they may have.

Coping with Stress—The importance of Control

So far I have discussed the biological and psychological characteristics of stress and some of the factors that affect how it is manifested. Much of what follows in the subsequent chapters of this book will be about *coping* with stress and trauma to help parents decide what do about alleviating stress and fostering resiliency. As a preamble to those chapters, I want to introduce one important guiding principle of coping—the feeling of having some control over both stressful events and the feelings that accompany them. As a broad rule, the more helpless a child feels in the face of stress and its aftermath, the higher his or her risk for psychological problems and the more difficult the recovery.

It was still dark outside when Julia came into our bed at

6:30 A.M. She told me that when she had awakened, her night-light was out. "But Daddy," she said in her most mature voice, "I didn't scream. I was jolted. But I got out of bed and came in here."

Julia was clearly proud of herself: She had stayed in control despite her fear. And rather than complain that she had woken me up earlier than I would have liked, I made a fuss over her.

"Good work! You didn't freak out. Excellent."

As the pale winter sun came up, we snuggled together and talked about her dreams and what the new day might bring.

In the weeks following 9/11, Julia had been afraid to go to sleep. She often woke up often in the middle of the night with nightmares of threatening monsters. No doubt these dreams were caused by 9/11 and the marauding soldiers in *Gone with the Wind*.

To help her control her stress, I borrowed a technique from the Senoi tribe, who live (or lived; the anthropological article from which this idea was culled was written in 1935) in the equatorial rain forest of the Malay Peninsula.[19]

Senoi children were taught by their parents that their dreams were important, not to be feared. They told their children that they had to take a responsible attitude toward their dreams, even while they were asleep. If a child was frightened by a dream in which he was falling, his parents would say that it was wonderful to have a falling dream and ask the child where he fell to and who he met there. If a child said monsters had appeared to him, he was instructed to be proactive—to befriend the monster if possible, attack if necessary, but never be frightened or run away.

In a somewhat desperate attempt to help Julia get to sleep one night after 9/11, I employed the Senoi strategy. If a monster frightened her in her dreams, I told her, she should approach it and ask it to play.

Lo and behold, the next morning Julia told me that she had had a talk with a monster in her dreams. "He agreed to play nicely with me," she said.

This method is not foolproof. Julia sometimes forgets to talk to the monsters—but the frequency of her nightmares has (for the time being, anyway) dropped since she adopted the Senoi strategy.

The wisdom of the Senoi strategy is that it teaches the child to try to take control of his fears. A related remedy for bad dreams is to install a "bad dream eliminator" or dream catcher over a child's bed. My version of a bad dream eliminator consists of batteries and old vacuum tubes left over from a guitar amplifier. I know other parents who use standard issue Native American dream catchers. I have heard of other parents who cast spells over their children's rooms. Some even go so far as to use magical incantations, incense, and garlic. Others post stuffed animal sentries at a scary door, closet, or window. These tactics all give the child a feeling of control and teach him to be proactive about his problems.

The lesson is much like the one President Franklin Roosevelt gave the nation in his first inaugural address. "All we have to fear is fear itself," Roosevelt said.[20] The greatest danger to someone facing stress is that he or she will become afraid and do nothing.

If one strategy fails to alleviate stress in your child, try something else. If, for example, a dream sentry fails to halt an intruding monster, the next night it should be replaced or at least told to be more careful. If the small dream catcher isn't getting the job done, make a bigger one. The important point is to keep working on the problem. A parent can also use emotion-focused strategies—methods that deal with the unpleasant emotions (e.g., anxiety, frustration, and sadness), not the problem that caused it. You can, for example, employ the useful advice of Maria in *The Sound of Music*: "Simply remember your favorite things and then you won't feel so bad." Over time, a child will begin to develop his or her own strategies.

One night in January when I was away doing interviews for this book, Julia asked her mother to lie down with her at bedtime so that she could go to sleep. Rather than immediately comfort her and comply, my wife, the psychologist, gave Julia a better alternative. Catalina's philosophy is that parents too often magnify children's fears by giving in to situations such as these. "It gives more power to the fear. It conveys to them that the fears are so big that they can't control them on their own."

Instead of getting into bed herself, Catalina offered Julia a pair of her pajamas to hold next to her as a kind of security blanket. The ingenious Julia filled the pj's to capacity with volunteers from her hefty stuffed animal collection and created a life-sized soft surrogate mother she could hold on to as she went to sleep. You can give your child a special pillow. You can rub his feet with a special "magic" oil that will protect and relax him. You can change the color of his night-light from white to red—a special red glow which, you can assure him, will protect him from harm.

_____

These examples show that a primary factor involved in successful coping is whether a stressful situation is perceived as controllable. James Henry, the eminent neuroscientist, discovered in his work with animals that if the stress to which an animal is exposed is something that it can easily handle, there will be an active coping response. During active coping, the neurotransmitters responsible for the "fight" side of the flight-or-fight mechanism will predominate.[21]

If, on the other hand, the stressful situation is perceived as overwhelming, an animal's anxiety will rise, and its coping strategy will become passive (e.g. fleeing or freezing). Levels of the stress hormone cortisol will increase. Chronically high levels of cortisol and similar steroid hormones cause brain damage. If the stress continues at an unmanageable level, over time the coping becomes so passive that the person or animal will not try to cope with the stress at all, even if the opportunity presents itself. With prolonged emotional trauma, our stress-regulation mechanism is thrown completely out of whack. It doesn't turn on at all. Cortisol levels return to normal and the animal is no longer reactive—it seems completely numb to stress. In animal experiments, this numbness may coexist with a kind of behavioral numbness called learned helplessness.

Learned Helplessness

Learned helplessness is induced in a rat by placing it in an experimental situation in which it receives moderate electrical shocks that come at unpredictable times and over which the animal has no control. Later, the rat is placed in a similar cage to the one in which it was initially shocked. But in this cage, there is an escape route. All the rat has to do now to avoid the shock is to jump over a low barrier, something that normal rats learn to do right away. The shocked rats, however, make no attempt to escape. They have learned to be helpless.

Humans in extremely stressful situations that they perceive as uncontrollable also exhibit learned helplessness. A woman who has been chronically abused over a long period and whose initial attempts to leave the abusive situation have failed may not try to extricate herself even if she is given the opportunity.[22]

One of the most beneficial lessons we can teach our children is to be resourceful—to not lapse into learned helplessness, an attitude that there is nothing they can do. We must empower them, give them the sense that they can make a difference. We'll see powerful examples of this lesson in the stories that follow in Part Two—children whose parents gave them the inner resources so that in adverse circumstances they didn't lapse into passivity and despair.

———————

As parents we need to know that our children will be able to face pressure and fear with humanity and courage when we're gone—and that they, in turn, will be able to pass these lessons on to their children. Teaching our children to be proactive, resourceful, and confident in dealing with stress is one of our most important tasks.

We should be proudest of our children not when they get straight A's on their report cards, but when they demonstrate courage and resilience in the face of adversity, when they show grace under pressure. Julia's control of her fear is a valuable indicator of the development of inner resources that will serve her well later in life. I will not always be there for her to crawl next to on a cold winter morning when she finds the night-light has gone out in her room.

In Part Three we'll talk about more ways in which we can help our kids deal with stress, but first I want to go to the stories in Part Two, and draw useful lessons about how we can help our kids transcend adversity, from the experiences of people who have endured hardships that most of us can't even imagine.

PART TWO

We have looked at some of the ways—for better or worse—that children respond to stress and trauma. They may regress, become sick, try to forget it, or draw support from friends and family. A child's coping style is determined by his age, temperament, and the techniques that he's learned from his parents—but it's also shaped by the culture and epoch in which he's grown up.

In this second section of this book, we present stories of strong children and the parents who helped make them strong. These are stories of the economic hardship of the Great Depression, the terror of the blitz bombings of London in World War II, the nightmare of the 1918 flu pandemic, the horror of the Holocaust, the oppressive fear of "the Troubles" in Northern Ireland, and the atmosphere of violence in Colombia.

The stories in Part Two add a human face to the scientific information presented in the last chapter. They are the real-life lessons about ways in which parents have helped to immunize their children against stress both before and during tough times. My hope is that we as parents will be inspired by these stories and pass the lessons we can learn from the past on how to be strong in hard times on to our children, who, in turn, will pass them on to their children.

CHAPTER 3

——

The Ties That Bind:

STRONG ATTACHMENT TO FAMILY AND COMMUNITY

Defenseless as babies are, they have mothers at their command, families
to protect the mothers, societies to support the structure of families, and
traditions to give a cultural continuity to systems of tending and training.
ERIK ERIKSON, *Insight and Responsibility*, 1966

Their names were Taco and Nacho—two cute tan and white
hamsters that my wife and I bought for Julia and Diana when
they were four and seven. This was before we had our cats.

Diana researched small rodents, so she was a hamster
expert by the time we purchased them. Julia fell hard for
Nacho, the smaller of the pair. She spent hours caressing him
and whispering sweet nothings in his ear. She introduced him
to all her stuffed animals and carried him through the house,
talking to him non-stop. He was her first love.

Diana was also enamored of Taco. Nacho's cage went into
Julia's room and Taco's into Diana's. I was pleased how

good the girls were about feeding and watering their new pets. What splendid lessons they're learning about responsibility and caring, I thought.

Then disaster struck. Nacho escaped.

Julia was in shock when she woke one morning to an empty cage. Nacho had always been a bit friskier than Taco. He had, we deduced, scaled the side of his cage and nudged loose its top. Diana immediately battened down Taco's cage top with books. Then she set about reading what to do when a hamster is lost.

We consulted with veterinarians, checked Web sites, and set non-lethal traps with peanut butter. Julia scoured the house, calling, "Nacho! Nacho! Come back, baby hamster." She was optimistic about his return. Diana had read that hamsters can carry two weeks of food in their cheek pouches, so Julia wasn't concerned that Nacho would starve.

Still, despite all our efforts, Nacho was gone. He seemed to have disappeared into thin air.

Julia refused to give up hope. "Maybe he's just exploring," she said. She thought, perhaps, that he had found his way back to his mother or moved in with a family of friendly mice somewhere in the walls of our house. Even after several weeks had passed, she remained convinced that he would magically reappear. Finally, we had to tell her that he wouldn't be coming back.

Julia was consumed by the loss. Her preschool teachers told us that almost all the pictures she drew were of hamsters. She had even shared her concerns about Nacho at morning "circle."

Understanding feelings was a big part of the preschool

curriculum, and the teachers decided to use Nacho's disappearance. Her teacher, Priscilla, told the class that Julia was missing her friend Nacho, and that sometimes those "missing Nacho feelings" made Julia sad.

"We talked as a group about feelings, and, in particular, sad feelings like Julia was having because she was missing Nacho," said Priscilla. "We asked what they could do to help Julia (or anyone else) who was having sad feelings. This led to a brainstorming session. The children came up with ideas—like giving Julia hugs, waiting for her when the class went to the music or art room so she wouldn't have to walk alone, and drawing pictures or making cards using kind words."

Soon, hamster drawings lined the walls, many with the word *Nacho* written in shaky preschool script. The teachers had put a card on the drawing table, spelling out Nacho's name. They also put out books on hamsters. Priscilla said that the kids sometimes used the classroom's playhouse to act out stories about Nacho.

"The children took an active role in helping Julia," Priscilla told me. "I think the fact that we formally acknowledged her loss gave the class the opportunity to express their feelings. Once the feelings were in the open and articulated, it created a healing atmosphere in the classroom for Julia and for us."

Boys and Monkeys

Human beings need social support during hard times. So do animals. Researchers have shown that infant monkeys who are put in a difficult situation—an unfamiliar cage, for example—experience more stress when they are alone or with strangers than when they're with monkeys they know.[1]

An analogous study of twelve-year-old schoolboys viewing a violent and disturbing movie yields the same result. If the boys viewed the movie at their own school with friends around them, their bodies secreted smaller amounts of stress hormones (catecholamines) than if they viewed the film at a different school in the company of strangers.[2]

All primates, including humans, are less anxious when they have a loving, supportive presence around them. Over the long term, that leads to better health. People with loving spouses, or close friends and family, tend to be healthier and to live longer lives. Children need parents. Adults need other caring adults. Studies have shown that social isolation is as big a risk to health as cigarette smoking or physical inactivity.[3]

People who are isolated (or isolate themselves) tend to have chronically high heart rates and blood pressure. In addition, they tend to have more intense cardiovascular reactions (e.g. higher blood pressure) to stressful situations, and, as a result, are more likely, over time, to develop heart disease. Their risk of dying is more than double that of someone who has at least one close friend.

Close friends also help prevent other diseases such as cancer. Biologists have found that social support is also associated with better functioning of the immune system, which is defined as the presence of more immune cells in the blood—more helper T cells, suppressor T cells, and natural killer cells.

The greater the number or relative percentage of these cells in the blood the better able the body is at fighting viruses and cancers. For example, in a study of women with breast cancer, those who said they had a person or close friend or partner who would listen to their concerns had more natural killer cells in their system than had women with lower levels of social support.[4]

Despite all this evidence that social support is healthy, scientists aren't sure exactly why it's healthy, or, for that matter, why social isolation is unhealthy.[5] There may be several ways in which having supportive friends and family help: They may encourage us to lead healthier lives, get more exercise or quit smoking, protect us from stress, or, most likely, soften the stress that we do experience. The most important aspect may well be the feeling we get from social support. Scientists continue to puzzle about the beneficial aspects of social support. It's hard to pin down what it is in a laboratory because it's a *feeling*. The sense of being connected is hard to describe exactly because these feelings existed before we had words to name them.

Early Bonding: The Foundation

The beneficial effects of social support can be traced back to the first family bond, which psychologists have traditionally referred to as mother-infant attachment (and, more recently, as a nod to dads, caregiver-infant attachment). Children who have a strong bond with a caregiver—a secure attachment—tend to be more competent; they are better problem solvers, and they have better relations with their peers, higher self-esteem, and fewer mental-health problems (such as depression and anxiety) than children with insecure attachment.[6]

When babies are afraid, fatigued, hungry, or stressed, they have several ways of coping, notably crying, clinging, or signaling their distress with a pleading look or reach. By six or seven months of age, the infant has learned to direct her signals for assistance towards specific, reliable caretakers—usually her parents. The infant recognizes these primary attachment figures. She seeks them out when she is stressed and aims the majority of her smiles and coos in their direction when she's not.

The infant with a warm, reliable parent who can read her cues and help soothe her comes to trust that her caretakers will be there when she needs them ("I got your back, baby"). With this trust comes the feeling of security a toddler needs to venture out and explore the world. A "home base" to return to gives the child the courage to take risks that are necessary for growth. In addition, when a caregiver soothes a distraught baby, when she helps her cope with the strong negative emotions that accompany her distress, the foundation is laid for the child to take over that role for herself.

Many parents, mothers especially, worry that they are jeopardizing secure attachment when they put their infant in daycare or return to work after what seems like too short a maternity leave. During the lifetime of the Millennials, the percentage of mothers returning to work before their children were a year old doubled, reaching an all-time high of 59 percent in 1998 (as of this writing the rate has dropped slightly, to 55 percent).[7]

In a recent article, Dr. Jeanne Brooks-Gunn (the hardest-working mother I have ever met), writes that the largest and most sophisticated national study of European Americans to date shows that when mothers returned to work before their child was nine months old, their children were less ready for school entry at age three than children whose mothers stayed home.[8]

This finding was not affected by the quality of the child's daycare situation, the quality of the home environment, or the mother's sensitivity to her child. The quality of daycare, home, and mothering were, of course, important for the child's welfare, but the findings concerning a mother's work schedule and school readiness remained even after taking these factors into account.

There was more bad news for some working mothers in the same issue of the prestigious child development journal that published Dr. Brooks-Gunn's article. In another large study, Israelis enrolled in daycare *centers* at an early age were more likely to be insecurely attached than children cared for at home or in family daycare.[9]

Parents must take many factors into account when deciding on how and where an infant will be cared for—the importance of career, financial needs, the quality of available care. In making a choice, we should consider the importance of the child's first and fundamental human connection. If her child's psychological health—including immunization against stress—were a mother's only concern, she would do nothing to jeopardize this early bond.

It's a shame that this country doesn't, in large part, have the government programs of paid maternity and paternity leave offered in other countries around the world. Parents in the United States are too often stranded, on their own. Other governments think that supporting parents is something that society has to contribute to ensure productive, stable citizens.

Insecure Attachment

What happens when early caregivers aren't reliable or are virtually nonexistent?

In the aftermath of World War II, many infants languished in orphanages. They tended to be touch-deprived. They had not been held, stroked, or cuddled in the way that all babies need. The term *hospitalism* was coined to describe the symptoms of disordered social relationships that was the legacy of this situation.[10]

Two types of relationship problems were observed in these kids. Some were highly anxious and vigilant—they were agitated, jumping at the slightest noise, always looking for signs of danger. Others tended to be indiscriminately friendly. I have often seen this phenomenon with older children in my clinical practice—kids whose parents were emotionally inconsistent or unavailable. They would, literally, jump into my lap at our first meeting. This was often followed by some not-so-subtle hints of wanting to remain with me.

After the overthrow of the Ceausescu regime in Romania in 1989, news reports circulated showing the ghastly conditions in state-run orphanages, affecting thousands of children. The few caretakers available to the infants were often indifferent to their needs. Bonding was not an option. Many of these Romanian children have been adopted into Canadian, American, and British homes—some as neonates, others much older—creating a ready-made laboratory in which to study the consequences of inadequate early attachment.

The prognosis for children with attachment disorders used to be bleak. But more recent research, such as the observations of adopted Romanian orphans, shows that recovery is possible under the right conditions. Children adopted into caring homes, with affectionate parents or caretakers who spend consistent time with their adopted charges, often develop normally.[11]

The consensus among attachment researchers is that although early attachment experiences are important for later psychological health, healing is possible if the growing child has positive social experiences, such as close friendships, neighborhoods where people regularly get together for activities such as meals, sports, or even car pooling, and caring school environments, where teachers are willing to focus individually on their students.[12]

Which brings us back to Julia, Nacho, and her supportive classmates.

Reach Out and Touch Someone

For Julia, the support in her classroom started on a tactile, visceral level—a hand to hold, a shoulder to cry on, a warm hug. Touch continues to be important for children long past the caregiver-infant bonding period (in fact, touch is important to our physical and psychological health through-out our lives).

At a physiological level, touch functions as a painkiller—for both physical and emotional hurts. When we are touched, our body releases endogenous opioids—the endorphins we associate with the runner's high. Those opioids relax us.[13]

The analgesic effect of touch also cues our body to slow down the secretion of stress hormones. As I mentioned in Chapter Two, these hormones help us deal with short-term stress, but when they're secreted over the long term, they can impair the immune system, cause ulcers and depression, and, in severe cases can, over time, cause brain damage, especially memory impairment.[14]

It turns out that one of the keys to "successful aging" is touch. Rats, like humans, often change as they get older. In particular, they develop memory problems; they don't learn to run new mazes as fast as they did in their younger days. Most of us over the age of forty can relate.

But some rats don't lose their memory as quickly as others.[15] If rats are handled—touched, held, stroked—for fifteen minutes a day during the first few weeks of life, over the course of their lifetime they secrete less stress hormones of the kind that can cause memory loss; in short, they're smarter as they age.

Dr. Tiffany Field and her colleagues at the Touch Research Institute at the University of Miami have been at the forefront of the touch movement. Their work has, for example, spurred many prestigious hospitals to provide mas-sage therapy to preterm infants confined to incubators.

Field illustrates how, compared to many other cultures,

America is a touch-averse society. Random snapshots of teenagers at a McDonald's in France, for example, show five times as many of them touching each other as a similar snapshot in an American McDonald's.[16]

Many school districts in America, fearing sexual abuse charges, no longer allow teachers to touch children. Julia, fortunately, wasn't in one of them—and the hugs she got from her teachers and classmates helped her cope with her first experience of death.

The Ten Best Things About Nacho

Feeling the need for closure, my wife and I proposed a kind of a memorial service for Nacho. With our help, Julia made a book, *The Ten Best Things About Nacho* (based on *The Ten Best Things About Barney*, by Judith Viorst). We wrote our memories of the departed hamster and made drawings of him. The book helped Julia accept that Nacho would not be coming back. Her teachers arranged for Julia to read the book aloud in class and showed her classmates our drawings.

Later that same school year, a boy in Julia's class lost his mother to cancer. The bond formed in the class over Nacho's death served them well for this far more serious event, and I was proud to see how easily my daughter made the switch from nurtured to nurturer. Julia's teachers had done an exceptional job of community building, of creating an environment where strong connections were fostered and support encouraged. I know all the children benefited from this environment.

I like to think of that class as an atom in the larger organism of our society. And I like to think that everywhere people are forming similar atoms in schools, places of business, houses of worship, and neighborhoods. In each such atom, parents and children draw strength and comfort from their connection to these groups.

Social Support Among Refugees

We Americans tend to think of ourselves as the strongest country in the world, and we are if military or economic might is the measure of strength. If, however, we measure strength by community cohesion or social support, we aren't even as strong as displaced persons living in refugee camps.

This, at least, is the observation of Dr. Theresa Stichick, a young woman whom I met when we both worked on a research study of families living in a wide range of Chicago neighborhoods. Some of these neighborhoods were socially cohesive. There were strong connections between neighbors and a sense of shared or collective neighborhood power. Other neighborhoods lacked this cohesion—neighbors didn't know each other well; they didn't rely on each other in times of need. They didn't know the names of the people who lived in the same floor of their apartment building.

For the last five years, Theresa has been working with children in refugee camps in Albania, Ethiopia, and Chechnya. She got her start setting up emergency education programs at the request of parents who had come to Kosovo to flee the fighting.

"They told me," said Theresa, "that since the fighting began, their kids had missed school. They were worried that their kids would fall behind academically—that they wouldn't be able to compete. The kids were anxious. They were having trouble concentrating. They were having nightmares. The parents were stressed out, exhausted, and needed help. They wanted to start up schools for their kids."

I asked Theresa about these families and whether she saw them disintegrating because of the intense stress they were under. I was surprised by her answer.

"In the countries that I've worked in," she said, "the role of the child in the family is very different than it is in the States. When it comes to social support around these kids in war, there is a circling of the wagons, a tightening of bonds, where people help each other, look out for each other, do things together. This is different from what I would expect to see in, say, kids in urban Chicago who don't feel that connection, who don't have that kind of social support, whose neighborhoods are anonymous. Looking at the survey data from Chechnya, almost every kid is off the charts in terms of how much social support he has. He feels that there are people who will take care of him. That he will have people who will help him if he needs help. That there are people he can talk to. You don't see very many kids thinking that they don't have the support of their families. But you do in Chicago."

I asked her if it was something peculiar about Kosovo. "No," she said. "It was like that in Ethiopia, too. It's the same way for every refugee group that I've worked with."

The Great Depression

This kind of communal support is something that we once were able to take for granted. Think of the millennia we spent in tribal societies—close-knit groups who suffered and rejoiced together. This need for community support is in our bones. When it's absent, we feel the lack.

What percentage of four-year-olds in Julia's preschool class will lose these all-important connections as they mature? Our millennial generation consists of children who are more likely to send an email or instant message to the kid next door, rather then make direct face-to-face contact. As we discussed in Chapter One, we are raising, in large part, an American generation that has learned to bowl alone.

The breakdown of this kind of social cohesion is a relatively recent phenomenon in much of America. Researching this book, I got a firsthand look at how most communities operated not so long ago when I went to visit Jane Brown, a nonagenarian in Anna, Illinois.

Jane was one of several people I interviewed who had lived through the Depression. I wanted to find out how that generation of Americans spoke to all of us who are searching for ways to raise resilient kids. There aren't many people still alive who were adults in the Great Depression. It's hard to imagine the immense doubt, fear, and confusion that gripped the nation in the winter of 1932–1933, the low point of the Depression, just before Roosevelt took office. There was widespread unemployment—perhaps 40 percent of the workforce. A two-year drought had destroyed farming in Arkansas, Oklahoma, Kansas, Colorado, and Texas, creating the infamous Dust Bowl. Two million itinerants—perhaps 200,000 of them boys under the age of fourteen—roamed the country looking for work. The homeless congregated in shantytowns along railroad tracks and riverbanks derisively called "Hoovervilles." One of these shantytowns, on New York's Upper West Side, stretched for a mile and half along the Hudson River.[17]

Yet for some families, Jane's among them, it was also a time when there was a strong sense of community and inter-dependence. This is part of what helped Jane's family and their friends survive.

Heart in the Heart of the Country

I went to interview Jane, to find out the secret of why her family had done so well when others had been devastated. I drove out of St. Louis across the Mississippi River into Illinois and then turned sharply south. The land was fertile, most of it in corn and soybeans. It began to roll, almost imperceptibly at first; the oscillations gradually became real hills. Then, in the tip of Illinois, forty miles north of the great confluence of the Ohio and Mississippi Rivers, I stopped in the small town of Anna.

Towns like Anna usually have a coffee shop where locals congregate before work, but many of its downtown brick buildings were boarded up, so I went to a McDonald's out by the highway for coffee and eggs.

As it turned out, that McDonald's was the local coffee shop. Everyone knew each other. Ten jovial men sat at a long table in the corner. Most of them were over seventy. The talk was about Holsteins, calves, and an acquaintance who had been kicked by a horse.

Not far from this group, an old woman in a faded blue stocking cap and a long coat sat alone, staring into a Styrofoam cup. If this were New York City, I'd have pegged her as homeless person, trying to warm up before she was shooed away for loitering. But, in Anna, each time one of the old men in the corner got up to leave, he stopped, patted her on the shoulder, and said something comforting. One of the men refilled her cup from the community coffee pot that sat on the counter. They clearly cared about her.

Even in the generic environment of McDonald's, I felt a clear sense of the community that existed in Anna. I couldn't imagine a similar scene in my own rather upscale neighborhood in suburban Boston. My town is too big, its residents too transient. When I go to my local coffee shop, even though the atmosphere is friendly, I usually don't recognize anyone. I was comforted and reassured that this part of America still existed—until I thought about Anna's moribund downtown and the age of the men who treated the old woman with courtesy and compassion.

"We Helped Each Other"

Jane's apartment was small and simple, neat as a pin, with framed photos of her family and hand-painted ceramic eggs scattered all around. One of her granddaughters, Mary Beth, an elementary school art teacher, had come to help with the interview, even though Jane made it clear she didn't need help.

Jane talked about life in the Depression. "Anna is a community that hasn't changed much in the last twenty-five years. But the people were even closer before World War II. Many of my friends are gone. But the younger generation here are still very close-knit and awfully nice to me."

"What was it like for you growing up here?" I asked.

She laughed. "Mother was born in Anna, so she had friends here. It was a community that didn't change much. Families stayed generation after generation until World War II. There were many families here who could trace their roots here to the 1800s.

"During the Depression, we used to make our own entertainment. It was very inexpensive. We had potluck suppers every Sunday night. We played bridge and just had fun together. We lived very inexpensively. People looked out for each other. We didn't feel the pain of it so much because we helped each other."

Jane explained that everyone felt strongly that Anna needed to take care of its own, from the people of the town itself to the farmers outside it. Because it was a small community, individuals were more prone to leap in and help when they saw a need. They pitched in together, sometimes burying past animosities, forgiving trespasses, and crossing party lines. Their ability to put aside their differences lessened the sting of the Depression for many.

"My grandfather, who was the mayor of Anna then— even before there was any federal assistance—set up a food pantry and clothes depot for the people in need," Jane said.

The teacher in Anna's one-room elementary school set up a face-saving hot-lunch program. She noticed that many of the farm children were so poor that they were coming to school with either no lunch, or lunches of cold biscuits and lard. She knew that the children and their families would resist anything that smacked of charity, so taking one parent into her confidence, she asked him (he was not having any financial difficulty) to buy a wood-burning stove. Then she approached some of Anna's food merchants for small donations: bones from the butcher, vegetables from the grocer, and any dairy from the creamery, and designed a "home economics project" for the students. She started every school day by having the students (usually the girls in particular) assess what kinds of food they had that day and then make a stew or soup, which would simmer on the stove all morning. At lunch everyone would eat the "project." She did this throughout the Depression.

During the thirties Jane pitched in by starting the first kindergarten in Anna. After reading about the benefits of early childhood education, she wanted to give a head start to the children in her own town.

The caring even extended to newcomers. After the war, about a dozen refugee families settled in Anna. Most of these were Jewish or Catholic families—both rare, exotic breeds in Anna—who were placed there as part of a federal program to help stir European expatriates into America's melting pot. I spoke with two women who were part of Anna's postwar immigrant wave, and they each reported that, despite their religious, cultural, and language barriers, they all felt embraced by the people of Anna. They remember Anna as a haven, and the years there as among the best of their and their parents' lives.

A friend of Jane's who was a nurse at the state hospital in Anna mentioned that some of the immigrants who worked there were having trouble dealing with the language barrier. Jane promptly started tutoring these hospital workers, one or two at a time. She felt that as an American she should do her part, and as a compassionate person she wanted them to have a good life here. She and her husband were invited to many citizenship parties as these men and their wives became American citizens.

Recalling the past as she had been doing during the hour and a half interview didn't seem to tire Jane. Rather she became energized. "I often think that a Depression wouldn't hurt us right now. It made me appreciate what I have. And I knew that I didn't need much in order to live. That it wasn't the material things that are important in life."

There was a resolute quality to Jane, a bracing lack of self-pity. She seemed sure of herself and capable. But there was also humility about her.

I drove away from Anna with Jane's words resonating inside me, mourning the passing of that community spirit that was once a part of America, a spirit which was once commonplace and gave our country so much of its character.

The Iowa Farm Crisis

At home, still under the spell of my day in Anna, I wondered whether I had overdosed on watching too many episodes of

Little House on the Prairie. So I turned to the work of Glen Elder, a seminal scientist in the emerging branch of psychology that combines child development research with historical analysis, for a more objective view of life in a small farming community. I was attracted to Elder's work also because it has some similarities with my own, especially in this book. He had recently investigated how families in central Iowa, many of them tied to farming and the land, had weathered the farm crisis of the mid-1980s.[18]

The Great Farm Crisis of the 1980s hit the American Midwest with the force of a tsunami. Many families who had farmed the same land for generations could no longer compete economically. Everyone knew someone who had lost his or her farm and left the state. Farm failures hurt non-farm business. Banks failed; stores and restaurants went out of business.

In tough times, family life tends to suffer. Children often feel less secure and need more parental attention, while parents, conversely, have less to give. They are less effective as parents—they tend to be irritable, harried, and depressed.

This was true for many American families during the Great Depression of the 1930s,[19] and it was also true for families in Iowa during the eighties. The stress affected nearly all central Iowa families, whether or not their livelihood was completely tied to the land.

Despite equal levels of economic stress, farmers' children tended to function better than kids in non-farm families. They maintained better grades (in my clinical experience, school grades are like the canary in the coal mine; their decline is often the first sign that a child has emotional problems). They had more self-confidence and were better able to maintain their social relationships than their peers.

What is it about farm life that protected these kids? The answer is that farm families tend to have more social capital than the rest of us. They have a richer web of interpersonal connections—involved fathers, grandparents, and strong ties to community. They drew on these connections during the Depression and the farm crisis.

Fathers

In the years preceding the Civil War—despite the growth of urban centers in the East and establishment of cities and towns that came with westward expansion—nearly 70 percent of American children grew up in two-parent *farm* families.[20]

One of the most important social aspects of farming was that fathers tended to be more involved in parenting than they were in non-farming families. With the advent of the Industrial Revolution, fathers increasingly commuted to work, and child-rearing responsibilities fell to mothers. But before this time, fathers were often the primary parent, meting out discipline and overseeing religious and moral education.[21] Even after the Industrial Revolution, farming fathers were more involved in parenting than non-farming fathers.

On a farm, every day is Take Your Child to Work Day. When children, boys especially, work closely with their fathers they tend to identify with and emulate them. This used to be more of the norm in America—the son would be an apprentice, learning his trade from his father.

It isn't possible for the average American dad to work side-by-side, day-to-day with his son, but it is possible to engage in other *shared* activities that help cement the bond they feel with us, to be part of our lives. Projects, camping trips, hobbies, travel, or simply walking and talking can provide some of the same benefits as planting corn together in the hot sun.

Too many American children are estranged from their dads. The emotional gap between them sometimes occurs because the dad spends too much time working, or because he's marginalized as a parent after a divorce, or sometimes simply because his spouse finds it easier (or less threatening) to do the bulk of the parenting herself. Studies show that adolescents are far more likely to confide in almost anyone (e.g. mothers or friends) than their dads.[22] And studies have also shown that boys who are alienated from their dads are at risk for a host of behavior problems, including substance abuse.[23]

Is there a difference between "fathering" and "parenting"? Yes and no. In general two parents are better than one—children receive more attention, each parent will bring unique skills to the mix, and the two parents can provide an important source of social and emotional support for each other. A father (as opposed to a parent) can also bring something special to child rearing. They may present a different style of nurturing than mothers typically do. Fathers can more easily be a role model for a boy, teaching a son about how to be man in this society—how to relate to members of the opposite sex, how to relate to other men, how to relate to work. Fathers can teach daughters something unique about how to interact with men, and, in stereotypical families, how to interact with the wider world.

I can't count the number of negative father-son relationships I have seen in my clinical practice and in my work as a school psychologist. The root cause, in my experience, is that the sons feel unloved. They feel their fathers don't respect them. These feelings often stem from the fact that the fathers and sons inhabit different worlds. They don't spend time together or share common interests. As a result, they don't really know each other.

Even today, the strong father-child connections that occur in many farm families are a source of strength, a secure home base from which to contend with life's difficulties. Spending long hours doing mutually meaningful activities together doesn't guarantee that a father and a son will become closer, but it is hard to see how they could become close if they don't spend this kind of time. My advice to fathers is to take the time to be with your sons (and daughters). Listen to them. Really listen. Learn what they like. Read their favorite books. Spend time getting to know their friends. Find out who they are. Don't abandon them to the world of their peers.

Grandparents

Elder's Iowa research found that involved grandparents are another important support for kids. Our children learn important lessons about developing moral character from their grandparents. In communities like Anna's, grandparents tend to be close by and help raise their grandchildren.

I asked Jane Brown's granddaughter, Mary Beth, what her grandmother had meant to her, especially during the hard times in her life.

"She and my grandfather have played a large role in my life," said Mary Beth. "I saw them constantly when my mother was a young student trying to study. My grandmother—I just think of her as the final authority on everything. She has such strength of character."

Mary Beth's early life was marred by intense emotional stress. Her parents were teenagers when her mother became pregnant. It was a shock to both families; this was the early sixties and this didn't happen in "nice" families. Mary Beth's mother became pregnant in part because she had left the fishbowl of Anna, where teenagers' actions were scrutinized by all the adults in the community. (One woman remembers that even when she was away at college her father would find out when her account was overdrawn because his office was next to the bank and he would get the news from bank officers as they met casually on the street.) As an older teenager, Mary Beth's mother spent considerable time away from Anna. She was enrolled in a kind of advanced placement program at a high school in Carbondale, a nearby college town, and fell under the spell of a fast, cool, dashing, and, as it turned out, domineering and violent boy. She was actually in the first semester of college, living at home, when Mary Beth was born.

She kept up an ambitious academic load when Mary Beth

was very young, as she worked toward first an undergraduate and then a graduate degree to prepare herself to be a teacher. Some of the time, she and Mary Beth lived near the campus in an apartment, some of the time they lived on the farm with her parents, who were very involved in Mary Beth's life—picking her up from nursery school, spending a lot of time with her.

Mary Beth's father was often unavailable, both physically and emotionally. He was physically abusive to her mother in the brief periods they tried to live together as a family, and Mary Beth witnessed scenes of violence repeatedly. "I remember one time he hit my mom so hard in the car, blood spattered all over all of us." While he never stuck her, Mary Beth remembers him as an impulsive presence full of anger—furious over little things like a child tripping and spilling something, or not moving fast enough. He would handle her roughly and almost painfully, and she believes one of the reasons her mother moved the two of them back to her grandparents' farmhouse was out of concern that he would turn his abuse more directly against the little girl.

When Mary Beth was almost four, she and her mother were living on the farm outside Anna as her mother prepared for graduate school exams. It was a Sunday morning. Her father had come to visit and then left, walking to his car outside. He shot himself once he got behind the steering wheel. Although she didn't see her father wounded (she was eating lunch in the kitchen when her mother discovered her father), she was aware of all the panic and haste with which her mother and grandmother leaped into the car to race him to the hospital. Her grandfather stayed with her, called ahead to the hospital, and then called other relatives nearby to come over right away. Jane supported the young man's bleeding head while her daughter drove, and she supported her granddaughter in the years that followed his death.

Despite the terrible event that happened there, Mary Beth's face lit up as she reminisced about being on the farm. She didn't associate it with her father's death, in part because her grandparents had always made her feel so safe. Nobody told her more than she needed to know about what happened to her father ("He went to heaven"), and the people she'd always relied on were consistent—her grandparents and her mother.

"It was just a wonderful place to explore," she said. "My grandmother always had art materials out for me. It was a much more organized and structured environment than I had at home. There was always a nice family dinner on Saturday night, and we would all go to church the next morning."

Mary Beth's grandmother was a safety net. Her home was a place to heal. One can only wonder whether Mary Beth would have done as well as she has in life if that net hadn't been there.

In addition to being a source of emotional support and a safety net, grandparents are, in the words of anthropologist Margaret Mead, "living proof that people can adjust."

Mary Beth's grandmother had experienced some hard times, such as the death of a child and her husband. "It was like the end of my world," she said. That her grandmother had survived these traumas gave her granddaughter a model for coping and the conviction that she could cope, too.

Unfortunately, the involved grandparent is another casualty of modern society. Despite the fact that a Millennial teenager is almost ten times as likely to have four living grandparents than a teenager born at the turn of the last century, fewer grandparents play a meaningful role in their grandchildren's lives.[24]

A Community of Overseers

Attachment to a wider community, as well as attachments to fathers and grandparents, is common in farm families. As one Iowa high school student said, "You know everybody. If something happens, you can interrupt someone at their house. . . . Most likely they know your parents or you know them."[25]

In the Iowa farm families Elder studied, both the men and women were more involved in the community than their non-farm neighbors. They felt more of a connection to place. They had been there for generations. They had roots. They joined the PTA and civic groups, and were more likely to be involved in a church. This not only created more community cohesion—a farm boy's father was more likely to be at the farm cooperative meeting with his classmates' fathers on a Thursday night than at home watching *Seinfeld* by himself—but also created social networks and connections that might help a child later in life.

When a teenager's parents know nearly everyone in the community, it's hard to get away with anything. As one Iowa farm boy said, "If I do something wrong, my father hears about it at the coffee shop next morning."[26]

This density of relationships—parents, grandparents, community—means someone is watching. Kids rarely spend unsupervised time. Children of full-time farmers spend less unsupervised time with peers and more in community activities such as 4-H church groups, and scouting—about two hours per week more than non-farm children.

Unsupervised teenagers can get into trouble. There is a peak of violent incidents during the after-school hours—3:00 to 6:00 P.M.[27] The highest proportion of teenage pregnancies gets started during these after-school hours as well.

As parents, we cannot take a hands-off approach to raising our teens. We cannot be too intrusive or dictatorial, but it's a mistake to be too trusting.

A member of a mother's group recently asked what to say when her teen asks, "Don't you trust me?"

"A parent should be feel free to say, 'No I don't.'" I replied. "I wouldn't have trusted myself at your age, and I'm not sure that I would trust anyone to resist the temptations that you may find yourself faced with. We are, after all, human."

After the Q & A, several of the women came up to me to get further justification for setting firm limits with their teens—not letting them stay home unsupervised at night or after school, stay out after midnight with their friends, or go to questionable parties. As we were talking, a young man who was in charge of the audio-visual equipment spoke up. "Dr. Kindlon's right," he said. "My parents never let me get away with anything. My curfew was always earlier than anybody else's. I was mad at the time. But now I know my parents knew what they were doing."

"There's the evidence," I said to the stunned group of mothers. "The old cliché is true: Someday they will thank you."

Conclusion

Families, friends, neighborhoods—a simple formula for building a strong foundation for your child. In today's world, however, it's often difficult to gather the right ingredients. In the end, it comes down to the choices we make, what we set as our priorities. Do you order a pizza and stay home to watch TV or make the extra effort to invite the new neighbors over for dinner? Do you ask your parents to visit on the Fourth of July—so that they can see your kids—even though they often drive you crazy? Do you take a job that doesn't require much travel, although it means a cut in pay, or become a stay-at-home parent? Do you enroll your seven-year-old in an intensive gymnastics program or do you take violin lessons together?

These are hard choices. As parents we all make them. But these days, when it comes time to choose, I remember Jane Brown's Depression-era potluck dinners, the farmer and his son harvesting corn together in the Iowa sun, and the old men of Anna coming together each morning for something far more important than a cup of coffee.

CHAPTER 4

———

Tough Times Call for Strong Parents

As we saw in the last chapter, when times are hard, it helps to have strong connections. Secure early attachments, social support, and community ties provide a secure base from which our children can draw when they're under pressure.

But our kids need more than this. They may need to be courageous in the face of danger, steadfast in periods of uncertainty. As parents, we all want to help them develop the inner strength that will see them through hardship, anguish, or loss. We want to know they'll be able to hold it together when their world seems to be falling apart.

How do our children learn to do this? In large part, by watching us, their parents, when we are under stress. We can draw a sense of how to act from kids who watched their parents live through periods of intense stress. History is full of examples of people who lived through tough times and exhibited grace under pressure. Each era has had its quiet heroes, average people caught up in extraordinary circumstances who—often with their children watching—rose to the occasion.

We don't have to look back very far in American history for these ordinary heroes. We can start with New York City, September 11, 2001, when nearly three thousand people were killed in the attacks on the World Trade Center—firefighters, venture capitalists, electricians, waiters, and bond brokers, who no doubt were devoted to their children. Some of these people left families who then had to try to fill the void.

Losing a Parent

I've seen children in my psychotherapy practice who have lost a parent. For most, if they get the care they need, the pain eventually subsides and they are left with only scars—the sign of a healed wound. When a parent dies, the child's adaptation is not merely to the event. The aftershocks—what transpires in the months and years following the loss—are usually more devastating than the death itself.

This became apparent to me in the case of David, a twelve-year-old boy who had lost his father to Parkinson's disease six months before he came to see me. David missed his dad; they had been very close. But he was slowly recovering, enjoying sports again, and doing reasonably well in school.

His mother, Elaine, however, was a different story. She became extremely anxious after her husband's death. Her husband had had lots of life insurance—but Elaine felt so financially insecure that she remarried only three months after I started seeing David. This sparked tension among her dead husband's relatives, ("She married so soon—can you believe it!"); and David's new stepfather, in his late forties, had never had children of his own. He had almost no warmth, and expected absolute obedience from his stepsons (David had two younger brothers).

Adapting to a new stepparent would have been tricky under the best of circumstances. But in David's case, it was a disaster. He and his stepfather never got along. His mom ended up in the middle, trying to support her new husband and keep him happy, while justifying to David why she had married such a "loser" (David's words, not mine).

I saw David periodically until he graduated from high school. His problems were never directly tied to grief over his departed dad; they were invariably about how his life changed for the worse after his father's death. I did what I could for him in therapy: providing emotional support, listening non-judgmentally, helping him think through solutions to his problems, helping him sort out his feelings about his mother and stepfather. I was one more piece of social capital in a life that had been turned upside down after the death of his father.

Hard Times Call for Strong Women

I am not judging David's mother. Adaptation to stress is idiosyncratic; recovery happens in different ways and at different speeds, but the stronger we can be in the face of danger or loss, the better it will be for our children. We need to try to be able to be there for them when they most need us. If we can do this for them, there's a good chance that they'll model our strength and ability to cope later in life, when they're on their own and faced with difficulties and challenges.

As parents we can learn lessons in coping and modeling strength for our kids from people who have lived through "interesting times"—the proverbial Chinese curse. Eighty-three years before 9/11, another catastrophe devastated New York City, leaving many young children without fathers or mothers. There are only a few people still alive who witnessed the catastrophe, and it is forgotten by almost everyone except those of us who work in public health.

The flu pandemic of 1918 was by far the worst public health epidemic in modern times.[1] Between October 12 and November 23 of 1918, an average of 460 New Yorkers died each day from influenza. All told, over 33,000 New Yorkers died over a six-month period. Boston and Philadelphia were hit even harder.

The best estimate of the total number of Americans killed by the flu epidemic is 675,000. At least 30 million died worldwide; some estimates are two or even three times that high. Paradoxically, the flu hit the healthy young adult population the hardest, and it left a disproportionate number of widows and orphans.

I wanted to see what lessons we could learn about stress and coping from the pandemic. It was a rare egalitarian affliction; its victims were not only the oppressed or downtrodden.

The flu pandemic had parallels to 9/11—it was an inexplicable, collective trauma that whacked a nation that felt invulnerable, basking in the self-assured glow of ascending greatness. It left many trying to rebuild their lives from the ashes and unsure whether the plague would return. How could people possibly cope? I wondered. How were orphaned children affected?

There are surprisingly few first-person accounts of coping with the flu pandemic. Katherine Anne Porter's novel *Pale Horse, Pale Rider* and *Memories of a Catholic Girlhood* by Mary McCarthy are the two of the most prominent. I was able to interview several of the few remaining witnesses. Some had escaped relatively unscathed, such as Jane Brown, who remembers the movie theaters in Anna, Illinois, being closed and her father not allowing the children out of the house during the worst of the flu. (In America, the flu moved from east to west and the public health response—non-existent at first—tended to improve as the danger was recognized.[2]) One theme emerged—strong women holding their families together in hard times.

Living Through the Plague

Marion, an eighty-nine-year-old woman who had lost her father to the flu, was a case in point. Her mother had persevered, showing incredible fortitude at a time when social pressures discouraged independence in women, and when women had far fewer opportunities than they do today. The social-service safety net was also far weaker then, full of holes.

I visited Marion at an assisted-living community in Denver, Colorado. She settled me on the couch. Religious pictures hung on the walls. Photos of children and grandchildren sat on end tables. A large window offered a gorgeous view of the Rocky Mountains.

Marion was six when the flu struck. Her father was thirty when he died. She described the flu epidemic. "It was shocking to see how many people were dying! There wasn't enough time to bury them all properly or get them to a mortician. There were so many funerals that, no matter whether you were Catholic or Protestant, there were no church services. There was no time. The morticians couldn't handle them all. My mother was desperate. My father had to go to the hospital. He was in the hospital for a week. Then he developed pneumonia. I remember the call when my mother got the news that he had died. They said he had been delirious and needed to be restrained—he was going to jump through a window. And I remember my mother just broke down. I wasn't allowed to go to the hospital. I knew that my father had died and I wanted to go with my brother and my mother to the funeral. But I had to stay at home with my godmother, and I remember the horse-drawn hearse going by the house, and I knew it was my father.

"Strangely enough, about six or nine months later, my father was exhumed because he was in a common plot, and my mother had bought another plot, so he was moved into another grave. For some reason, my mother wanted to see him once more. I have a real good picture of my father: He had sort of chestnut-colored hair, like mine. They opened the coffin and you could see his hair blowing in the wind.

"When I was with my godmother during the funeral I had

thrown a tantrum, kicked a hole in the wall. She tried to pacify me. I felt so bad. I think that's why my mother allowed me to go see him again. And I think that helped me finalize the event."

Marion went into the kitchen to fill up my water glass. She refused to let me get it even though her arthritis made it painful for her to stand up.

"Do you remember how your mother helped you deal with your father's death and the death that was all around you?" I asked when she returned.

Marion paused then looked up at me straight in the eye. "My mother was very industrious," she finally said. "She decided that she was going to provide for her children no matter what. Perhaps that's why she married so soon after she was widowed. My father's brother wanted her to put us in an orphanage, because, he said, there was no way she could take care of us." Marion's tone was dismissive. "But my mother went to work in the foundry where my father had worked. She got a friend of hers from the foundry to stay with us at night because that's when she went to work—the night shift. I remember her coming home in the morning in black coveralls. No matter what, we always had food on the table."

I took a sip of water and glanced at Marion, sitting ramrod straight despite her arthritis. "She sounds like a strong lady! That must have affected you. Do you remember anything specific? Did she say that this is what people have to do? That they have to pull themselves up?"

Marion nodded. "My mother always felt that there was a way to survive no matter what the circumstances. And that really stuck with me. That first Christmas stands out for me. It was less than two months since my father had died. Even though we were in tough financial straits, my mother had the wherewithal to find a social worker at the Catholic Charities to bring over a big basket of goods—fruit and things. Children didn't expect scores of presents the way they do today. It really impressed me that my mother had been able to get that for us. My father had been the provider, but I saw that my mother was intelligent enough and had the grace and the strength to say, 'I'm going to keep my family together.' And that really carried me through my own life. That stayed with me: that there always is a way to live. There is a way to cope with situations no matter how hard it is.

"I thought about my mother's example when I was raising five children during the war [World War II]. That was no easy feat. My husband was at sea for months at a time. But I always felt there was a way. I always had courage, even when we were in financial straits. I thought of my mother. She passed along to me her energy and optimism. I always felt that I could cope. And those lessons have stayed with me all my life."

The Visual Cliff

Marion learned from her mother to be strong and determined in times of crisis, instead of falling apart. Psychologists in the later part of the twentieth century began to study how traits of perseverance and fortitude are passed from mother to daughter. We have gathered a great deal of information about how children, even as infants, learn to react to emotional situations.

Some of what infants do is reflexive, of course. Babies are naturally afraid of very loud noises, for example. No normal ten-month-old would wittingly crawl off a cliff. Or would he?

The brilliant Cornell researcher Eleanor Gibson invented an apparatus—the "visual cliff"—to study exactly that question. The cliff looks like a large square glass table. There is a checkerboard pattern underneath the glass, which, on the cliff's shallow side, is right under the glass and looks pretty much like a tiled kitchen floor. On the deep side of the cliff, the checkerboard pattern under the glass is nearer the floor, creating the illusion of a cliff.

Gibson first used the visual cliff apparatus to demonstrate that young infants have depth perception—they won't crawl over the "cliff" from the shallow side to the deep side, even if their mothers encourage them. The infants instinctively know to be wary of the drop-off.[3]

But how do children learn in more ambiguous situations, which make up the bulk of their experience? How do they figure out whether to be afraid of bugs, snakes, dogs, strangers, or vacuum cleaners?

Gibson and others showed that children look to their parents and other adults for cues, a process psychologists have called "social referencing."

An ingenious group of researchers used Gibson's visual cliff to demonstrate social referencing. They raised the floor of the "deep end" of the cliff. It left enough of a drop so that nearly all the infants tested were too wary to crawl over it on their own. But because it was ambiguous, the infants looked at or "referenced" their mothers frequently, as if to ask, What should I do?

The researchers found that they could make the infants crawl over the cliff under certain conditions. If the mother showed an expression of fear or anger, almost no infant would cross over to the other side, but if she showed happiness or interest, nearly all the infants would cross.[4]

Social referencing for children happens in all ambiguous situations. Nearly all parents of toddlers have had the experience of being with their child when she falls down. If the fall isn't a bad one—that is, if the child isn't in significant pain—she'll look up at her parent with a look that seems to say, "Am I hurt?" "Should I be scared?"

The child takes her cue from the parent. If the parent looks scared, so will the child. If someone falls down in front of the child, she will look to her mom to see what her expression is. Does her mom laugh? Does she look concerned? Does she try to help? Researchers who study the development of empathy find that kids model their parents. If the parent shows empathy, so will the child.[5]

This kind of social referencing between parent and child takes place thousands of times over the course of childhood. And it carries over to the child's experience of similar situations even when the parent isn't around. In another experiment, researchers exposed one- to three-year-olds to unfamiliar toys. The infant looked to the adult for cues. The experiment was designed so that each toy was accompanied by a different facial expression on the adult's part.

When the kids were shown the toys again, they responded to them based on their past referencing. If the toy had been shown to them and the adult looked fearful, the next time the child saw the toy, even if there was no adult reaction this time around, he was more likely to be afraid of the toy and shun it.[6]

A variant of social referencing extends to feedback about the child's own behavior, notably when the child is expressing negative emotions. Research shows that if a parent typically responds to a child's distress (if a child cries when a toy breaks, for example) with distress or discomfort ("I can't stand to see her cry so much") or anger aimed at suppressing the emotion ("Stop crying, there is nothing to be upset about!"), the child tends to grow up to be less socially competent.[7] Specifically, he is more likely to have trouble maintaining friendships and is more likely to act in counterproductive ways in emotionally laden situations.

A child will tend to be more socially competent if a parent typically responds to distress with support ("Oh, you're so sad, tell me what happened"), or, more importantly, with problem-focused responses ("Let's see if we can fix it"). The child learns to recognize his emotions when he's stressed. He learns not to deny his feelings, but to regulate them. His feelings don't overwhelm him.

We have to model for our kids that we can handle stress—that problems can be solved. Studies of children who have lost a parent show that the key to recovery was having a mentally and physically healthy surviving parent. We need to let our children know that we can rise to meet challenges. We need to show them how to be strong. This kind of modeling will pay off in the long run, as the next story illustrates.

Prudence Paine and the War in England

From August 1940 to May 1941, the Luftwaffe conducted a series of nearly daily air raids against southern England, called the "Blitz," from the German word for lightning. During the height of the Blitz, London was attacked for 127 consecutive nights. In addition to high explosives, the German bombers also dropped incendiaries—bombs filled with highly combustible material such as napalm or oil that were designed to create firestorms. These types of bombs were dropped by the British and Americans later in the war, causing heavy civilian casualities in cities such as Dresden and Tokyo.

Then, after the Nazis abandoned the idea of invading England, they continued to rain terror on British cities and towns with "Vergeltungswaffe" or "retaliation weapons," a flying bomb and early guided missile whose names were quickly shortened to the V1 and the V2. My father, who was in London to recuperate after being wounded, remembers V1 buzz bombs coming over the hospital where he was recovering. "Those things scared the hell out of me. The buzzing would stop and you knew it was coming down, but you never knew where it was going to hit."

All told, 30,000 British citizens died from German bombs, including 800 firefighters, who often worked while the raids

were in progress. Tens of thousands of civilians were seriously injured and hundreds of thousands of homes were
destroyed.[8]

Prudence and her Mother During the War

Prudence is the director of the afternoon program at Park
School outside Boston. I drove to see her at the school on a
beautiful Indian summer day. I found her in the staff room.
She is a thin woman who smiles easily. Although she has
lived in the United States most of her life, her voice still
retains a soft English accent. She carries herself with a quiet
dignity. But she is not reserved when she discusses her past.

I particularly wanted to know how her mother had
parented Prudence through the stress of wartime and the
bombings. Although Prudence didn't grow up in London
proper (her father's vicarage was in Kent, about twenty miles
closer to the coast), she and her mother had firsthand experience with the Blitz.

Her mother had raised Prudence in large part alone after
Prudence's father, a minister and then army chaplain, had
been killed by a stray shell on a Normandy beach while tending to the sick and the wounded.

"Do you remember your father's death?" I asked her.

Prudence let out a barely perceptible sigh. "I remember
it as if it were yesterday. We were in Gloucester, which is a
long way away from Kent, staying with my aunts in the country. And I was alone with my mother in the house. The tele-
graph boy came on his bicycle and gave my mother the
telegram. She just said, 'Thank you very much.' Of course,
everybody lived in dread of that moment. She told me to go

and get a certain picture book. It was a grown-up book with artwork. She went over to the sofa and sat me down next to her. And we looked at it together. I don't actually remember her saying to me that my father had been killed. I do remember that when my aunts came home my mother was completely grief-stricken. I was not allowed to be with her for almost a week. She went to bed, and I was kept away. But other than that one lapse, my mother was a pillar of strength throughout the war."

So much so, in fact, that despite the personal danger they were in from the bombing, Prudence's memories of the war are, for the most part, pleasant.

"My mother made it fun for me and that's what I really stress," Prudence said. "I never got the feeling that it was a dangerous time. I didn't feel deprived of anything. I remember going to ballet school. My tutu was made from tissue paper. We still played games and read together. It didn't matter; it was fun. My mother didn't feel the need to tell me what was going on. She didn't share the danger we were in until I was quite a bit older."

Prudence was about six years old at this time. It was wise of her mother to protect her from an awareness of the full extent of the danger they were in.

Prudence continued. "I remember one night when my mother took me to a hill overlooking a valley. 'Prudence,' she said, 'do you see the lights in the valley?' I remember they looked like fairies to me, but they were incendiaries, of course. We were in a little village, but there were searchlights. In the field next to us, we had a barrage balloon."

"Were you ever bombed?"

"Yes. One night, we saw this rocket coming. It looked to me as if it missed the church tower by about an inch. I couldn't believe it! I knew, although I was only five or six, that something wasn't quite right. Another time, we were staying at my grandmother's out in the country and a V2 bomb landed in the driveway. I remember that we had glass all over our bed because the windows had come in. It was winter. It was snowy and we had to evacuate the house. My mother went around, gathering everybody up. There was glass all over the floor, nothing on her feet; she never got cut at all. She dressed me in the little pretend leather airman's suit that I loved. My grandfather wouldn't leave until he found his teeth. The dog had puppies two days later and the cat went up a tree for a week.

"We walked down the driveway in the dark in the snow across the road to a school. And they hadn't heard it. That was the extraordinary thing about a V2. You didn't hear it if you were close to it. They had heard it two villages away and thought it was miles away, so they didn't bother to send anybody out."

Prudence smiled as she related the story.

"You make it sound like it was fun to have your house bombed," I said.

"In some ways, it was. I just remember all the good things. It's an interesting thing that my mother remembers how hard it was and how worried she was about me. But I don't remember that at all. I don't remember being unhappy—ever. I suppose there was some fear, but I didn't see it."

Prudence's mother fits the stereotype of the stoic wartime

Brit, "doing her bit," with chin held high, resolute gaze, and stiff upper lip. This heroic cultural portrait—enhanced by wartime movies such as *Mrs. Miniver* (Best Picture, 1942)— is part propaganda, created for a hard-pressed nation. It does, however, have a basis in fact. There were many real-life Mrs. Minivers who, like Prudence's mother, were able to "get on with it" despite the difficulties they had to endure.

"How did she make you feel happy and secure?"

Prudence thought for a moment. "She was never nervous. I never saw her cry. What she did privately, I don't know. I always felt safe, very safe. She never transmitted her fear to me. She always stressed that we were together and that was what was important—that we were all together. She didn't let me know that there was something terrible going on. I was very aware that on September 11—we were working here—we weren't supposed to tell the children what was going on. That was up to the parents to do. Most children went home early, but it was horrible for us because we had to be the best actors in the world, pretending that we were having a normal day and that everything was fine. That's what my mother must have done, day in, day out. The strain must have been horrible. But I have tried to emulate her great resilience. I thought about her when I had the traumas in my life."

It was hard for me, a psychologist, to ignore the word "trauma."

"You say you had traumas in your life. What do you mean by that?" I asked.

She hesitated. "Our youngest child was killed in a car crash at age twenty in 1987," she finally said. "He was up at

Dartmouth for the summer semester. He was the only one killed. There were four people in the car. He was in the backseat. They weren't drunk. They were probably going too fast and he didn't have a seatbelt on. The puppy he was holding survived. My husband had been on sabbatical for six months in Europe. We had just come back for our twenty-fifth wedding anniversary, which the children were planning to give us. And then four years ago my husband walked out on me. No warning. After thirty-six years. I went to get my hair cut, came back and he had gone. He's remarried now." She continued: "My mother's example helped me. Certainly when my son died her influence on me was huge. The way she had carried on. She taught me that life continues. After our son died, I remember going to the supermarket by myself (at the beginning I couldn't even do that by myself) and I wanted to scream, 'Stop doing what you're doing. Don't you know what's happened!' And then it slowly dawned on me that everybody's got something difficult to deal with. You're not alone. It may not be as traumatic as a child's death. It may not have happened yet. But before they die they're probably going to face something that's pretty horrendous. It could be their own illness. It's something that you realize and puts things in perspective. You start realizing how lucky you are. I've had some real bum raps, but I'm so lucky."

"What are you thankful for?"

"My children. They are precious to me. I'm thankful my mother is still alive, although she's ready to go on to her next adventure. And I feel thankful for all my incredible friends. And I had a wonderful counselor when my son died. I never thought as a British person of ever going to a counselor, but

I had another friend who had two children die and she said, 'Get help.' And so I did. My friends, children, and counselor. That's the reason I'm here. I wouldn't be here otherwise."

"Do you always try to emulate your mother?"

"There were some things I wouldn't emulate. I think I'm more affectionate and loving towards my children than my mother was to me. She was very loving, but she wasn't as understanding sometimes. I think mostly what I've emulated in her is her great resilience. And I thought that when I had the traumas in my life I would be letting her down in some way if I didn't try to do as well as she had. She was a model for me."

"I can't think of any greater gift a mother can give a daughter," I said.

Prudence profoundly impressed me. At some level, she and her mother made me feel ashamed. I recalled times when I wasn't such a great model for my kids: instances where I reacted to petty annoyances—traffic jams, broken computers, children's chores unfinished—as if they were traumas. Prudence reminded me that in each of these instances of unregulated emotion, my children were watching and learning. Part of being adult is being able to handle petty annoyances with grace and equanimity. If we do so, it is more likely our kids will, too.

Divorce Is Worse than Death

Death is not the only way a child can lose a parent—a far more common way is through divorce. Of the 70 million children in the United States, only 50 million live with both parents. Most of the rest—close to 17 million—live only with their mothers. Fourteen million of these women have lived with a husband at one point, but have become (or have chosen to be) single mothers. Less than a million of them are widows.[9] Because being widowed is relatively uncommon, most of what psychologists know about how children and adolescents cope with parental loss comes from research and clinical experience on divorce and separation.

Children who have lost a parent to either divorce or death are at risk for a host of behavioral problems including low grades, low self-esteem, and problems relating to peers, siblings, and parents. The risk for these problems is higher for children of divorce than for children who have lost a parent due to death. Overall, children whose parents are divorced are about twice as likely to develop emotional or behavioral problems as a child in a two-parent home.[10] These kids tend to have more stress and less support.

To be sure, children grieve when a parent dies. In some cases, the grieving will overwhelm the child and he will develop a psychiatric disorder, such as clinical depression. But, overall, the long-term risks to mental health are very small compared to what can happen after a divorce.[11]

I've seen scores of kids who have dealt with divorce. For many years I ran a therapy group for boys whose parents were divorced or separated. In many instances, the father became a shadow figure, either disappearing altogether from the child's life, or popping up erratically. Too many times I've had boys tell me (desperately trying not to cry) that their father hadn't shown up for a ball game as promised or forgotten to send a birthday card—again.

One of the main reasons that divorce is usually harder on kids than the death of a parent is its aftermath. There is no one example of a bad divorce. To paraphrase Tolstoy: Good divorces are all alike; each bad divorce is bad in its own way. The worst-case scenario for a child is when the acrimony between parents spills over into the child's life—when, in the psychologist's parlance, the child is "caught in the middle."

A six-year-old boy once drew me a picture. His mother was rendered on one side of the big manila sheet, his father on the other. The boy drew himself in the middle on his bicycle, unsure of which direction to ride.

Another time a nineteen-year-old girl came to me for advice. She was an only child, and her parents had divorced when she was still in elementary school. Now that she was in college, her parents were each going to remarry. "They both picked the same wedding date," she whined, suddenly sounding much younger. "Which wedding should I go to?"

"You can't be serious." I shot back. "If it were me, I wouldn't go to either." I never found out what she decided, but I hope she followed my advice if her parents didn't change their selfish, manipulative behavior.

There are many more examples of a child caught in the middle: arguments over tuition, child support, custody, visitation, bedtime, diet, sports participation, and exposure to the ex's new lover.

In a divorce it is often extremely challenging for people to be strong, to maintain their equanimity and emotional intelligence—to show a measured reaction to an ex's misguided child-rearing technique, lifestyle, or lack of financial and emotional support.

In the majority of cases, it is the woman who has to display the most strength. The children tend to give her a harder time. Children, in my experience, tend to believe that their mother won't abandon them, but they are not so sure about their dads. In many instances, they don't get to see their fathers as often, so they are often nicer to them as a result and will work harder for paternal affection (nothing makes us want something as much as when it looks as though it might be taken away from us).

For these mothers, swallowing the anger and vindictiveness that can often follow the trauma of a divorce is the hardest thing they'll ever do. I have seen many who have done it well for the sake of their children.

All parents need to remember that when the marriage has ended, parenting goes on. Changes in economic circumstances, different standards of living, stepfamilies, and new parental love interests are stressful for children. Their parents need to do whatever they can to be as strong, understanding, and compassionate as possible.

Preexisting Conditions

It isn't only what happens after a trauma such as divorce or parental death that affects whether a child will successfully adapt. Preexisting conditions are also important. A child who is anxious, for example, will be at greater risk for developing problems following a loss than the well-adjusted or less timid child.[12]

The child's age at the time of the stressful event—as we've discussed in Chapter Two—may also be important. Younger children, because they are more dependent than older kids, will be more anxious about being abandoned. A parent's strength for these children should go toward creating a normal atmosphere by maintaining the energy to do normal activities, even as she is depressed or reeling from having her husband walk out on her.

Adolescents and older children often need a parent to be strong enough to show emotion without being too demoralized. They need to see us as strong enough to help them deal with their emotions. Interviews show that many adolescents are reluctant to talk with a widowed or divorced mother because they think she won't be able to handle it. Others, especially older girls, get a boost in self-esteem when they are called on to take on more adult responsibility. They rise to the occasion, and these girls often develop very close relationships with their mothers.

If, however, the challenge of more responsibility is too great or the relationship with the mother becomes too close, not allowing the daughter enough room to develop as her own person, the results can be awful: high levels of family tension, depression, and diminished self-esteem. Thus, for the most part, it is best for the parent to maintain her role to be the strong, secure home base that allows the child to remain a child.

A person can only be so strong. Sometimes parents try to make superhuman efforts to be strong, but end up with the opposite result; they fall apart. Instead of being more available for their children, they become less so. Everyone has a limit, and it is a wise person who knows what those limits are.

La Violencia

I contrast my upbringing with my wife's. She grew up surrounded by violence in Bogotá, Colombia—the great-great-granddaughter of a man who had been elected to Colombia's presidency (and assassinated before he could take office).

To get a sense of Colombia, imagine an America in which an anti-government organization (think Timothy McVeigh) is so powerful that it has complete control over a large chunk of northern Montana. Imagine further that this organization is in league with and receives large cash infusions from an enormous organized crime syndicate. This would be an America where a few years earlier the Supreme Court building in Washington, D.C., was attacked and most of the justices were killed. It would be an America where five U.S. senators and congressmen are being held for ransom, where kidnapping of affluent citizens is big business, and where the life expectancy of honest policemen and committed journalists is short.[13]

Colombia is one of the longest-standing democracies in South America, but disputes between its liberal and conservative parties have often erupted into violence and civil war. When liberal leader Jorge Eliecer Gaitán was assassinated in Bogotá in 1947, riots broke out and the city's center was left in ruins. Fighting spread to the countryside and continued into the mid-1960s. During this period, called *La Violencia,* about 200,000 Colombians were killed, primarily in the countryside. This atmosphere of violence affected Catalina as a little girl when she visited her family's *finca* or country home (most affluent Colombians have a *finca*).

Her father, an engineer, bought a *finca* that was a three-and-a-half-hour drive from Bogotá over winding mountain roads. It had a hundred acres of land, and about fifty head of Swiss and Holstein cattle and riding horses. It grew guavas, pineapples, and mangos. It supported itself, but it wasn't meant to be a business.

The *finca* was near the mountains where Marxist rebels lived. The rebels would frequently come down out of the mountains and attack landowners, kidnapping or killing them. Even though this happened to families nearby, Catalina said she never felt in any danger because of the confidence her father inspired, the way he projected an air of normality into what was a risky situation.

I recently asked Catalina to tell me again about her girl-hood in Colombia, one night after we had put the kids to bed.

"How did your father convince you that the farm was safe?"

"My father inspired tremendous confidence. It wasn't only the farm that was dangerous! On the way to the farm, I was remarkably unafraid as he passed car after car on the narrow road. It was sport for him, seeing how many cars in a row he could pass at one time. Eleven was the record. My brothers and I never thought for a moment to question his judgment. That was the kind of confidence he inspired. He

105

explained to us that we only traveled to the farm during the day because the rebels only attacked using the cover of darkness. He said our town was safe. And we believed him! In neighboring towns, there were frequent incidents. *Haciendernos* (landowners) were killed. They were not just killed—they were massacred, their arms, legs, and heads chopped off with a machete. Two notorious rebel leaders in particular I remember: *Sangre Negra* (black blood) and *Tiro Fijo* (sure shot). They modeled themselves after Che Guevara. Violence was all around us. Colombia has the reputation as the most violent country in the world—and I would certainly not dispute that. There were often reports of killings that I was aware of when I was a child. And then there were cockfights and bullfights. I know I've told you that I went to the bullfights! My father and brothers hunted. There were rifles and guns in the house."

"What about when violence came to your doorstep?"

"The closest violence ever came was when we were robbed. The maid opened the door to a huge bouquet of flowers. Nothing extraordinary in that. My mother frequently entertained. But behind the flowers were men with machine guns. One smashed a rifle butt into the maid's head, knocking her out, and in they stormed. My mother, napping upstairs, heard the commotion and tried to escape out the back door. But a bandit with a gun was waiting for her. She wrestled with him—a ridiculous image, as you know, since my mother is so petite and prides herself on her elegance. A maid from across the street came running toward them. My mother's assailant shot the woman in the leg. My mother managed to escape, but all our silverware was stolen. No one thought much about it. This was an everyday event in Columbia—*La Violencia*, the state of things.

"It is still hard to believe that you could feel safe in such an environment."

Catalina laughed. "It's hard to explain. It was because of who my father was. He was everything to me. I felt he could keep me safe no matter what. Sometimes just the two of us went to the farm. He drove skillfully around hairpin turns. But he took calculated risks. For example, he would wait for a straight section of the road and remove his sweater, first taking his arms out of the sleeves and then telling me to pull the sweater over his head. The musty smell of Piel Rojas (red skin) cigarettes that he smoked was strong in his clothes and hair. As we drove he told me stories. In one he was drilling for oil in the jungle near the border with Venezuela. He couldn't find his way out of the jungle and had to spend the night in a tree. 'Tilín, Tilón,' he said to me, using my nickname. 'It was dark and I couldn't get back to camp. There were jaguars around, and I figured I would be safest in a tree. So that's where I slept.'

"I took his exploits as a matter of course. I had the feeling that no matter what the danger, he'd figure out what to do. He was infinitely resourceful. He made my brothers and I feel that way, too. He taught us everything. He taught us that we had the resources to take care ourselves. He taught me small practical things. How to change a tire, for example. For a girl in Colombia that was an anomaly. He projected competence. He put an emphasis on education. He told us: 'People can take anything from you except what's inside your head. The revolution can take everything from us. But it can never take what you've learned, your expertise.'

"That sense of competence enabled me to live in Paris by myself for a year when I was sixteen, and then pack my bags, leave home, and go to Harvard for college. It saw me through graduate school. And, you know, it helped later, during that horrible year when Katie was stillborn, my brother was killed in a car accident, and my father died following surgery. But most of all it allows me to specialize in trauma work in my practice. I think that by not being freaked out when my patients recount some of the truly horrific experiences they've had, I give them courage, a sense that someday they might be able to be at peace with their memories."

"Given your background, what was your reaction to 9/11?"

"I felt the initial shock of it like everyone else. And I have great empathy for the survivors and victims' relatives. I can understand that many of them were traumatized by the events. But, I must say, I was amazed at the general American reaction to 9/11. Most Americans I know seem to have trouble living with the idea of a constant, incipient threat. Many of my patients have become anxious; they have trouble sleeping. But 9/11 hasn't fazed me. It's not that I'm being unrealistic. I know this will be with us for years. I know there will probably be more attacks. Still, the environment here is so much safer than the one in which I grew up. That was why after I obtained my Ph.D. and the best university in Colombia offered me a job in their psychology department, I declined it. There was no way I would go back to live in Colombia and *La Violencia*."

"So, you mean, the threat is relative?"

"Yes, that. But more than that. I feel a calm acceptance around the events of 9/11. Violence where I grew up was random and endemic. It can't stop you from living. Now, when we're at a public event, I take note of where the exits are, in case something happens. Beyond this my life and mood hasn't changed. I think it was a form of arrogance to think this kind of thing wouldn't happen here. This kind of threat is what much of the rest of the world has been living with. Horrible things happen in the world. Death is all around us. But we need to affirm life. Terror will keep happening. But to live in fear all the time is not the best way of coping. You have to be able to set it aside and live life. We can't have fear curtail our activities—stop us from traveling, stop us from enjoying ourselves. You know, we've discussed this. I've asked Diana how the events of 9/11 have affected her. She answered as I hope most people would answer. She said the events had not affected her directly and that future terrorist actions were probably not going to touch her. Another, more pessimistic response—that we have to watch out, that our lives are in danger—makes life infinitely more stressful and difficult than it needs to be. If we convey that to our children, their development will be affected. We cannot lead them to believe that danger lurks around every corner. I think parents made a mistake to sit their kids in front of the TV after 9/11 and have them watch the WTC fall again and again. It makes it much more traumatic than it needs to be."

———

I agree with my wife. It is important for parents to remember that part of their job is to convey to their children that a situation, no matter how frightening, is manageable. This doesn't mean that we shouldn't teach our kids to be cautious. Indeed, teaching caution is sometimes the best way to manage a frightening situation. But we must not convey that we are afraid to act. Recently, I was part of a panel of child psychologists at a convention for summer camp directors. One of them asked us what we thought was the best way to handle the 9/11 fallout with this year's batch of campers. The first psychologist's response was, "Let the kids know that we're afraid, too."

I had to disagree. "It is all right to let children know we are afraid," I said, "as long as we also tell them that we are confident that we have the situation under control. We can do this by keeping to our routines, by keeping calm and positive." Catalina's father was a master of this. He projected confidence and protected her from a fearful childhood. His gift has helped her cope with all the traumatic events in her own life and help trauma victims overcome their fears.

Lessons from the Past

History has been kind to people like me who have lived in relative peace and security throughout their lives. I fervently hope that my children and their children's children continue to enjoy this kind of blessed existence. But, as Prudence reminds us, it is almost inevitable that someday we will all "have to face something pretty horrendous." One of the most interesting aspects of my interviews with elders who lived through catastrophes such as the flu pandemic, the Great

Depression, and World War II was their reluctance to complain about their lives.

I interviewed three widows in Fort Worth, Texas, all born in the early part of the century. They all sounded the same theme: Life may have been hard, but that was just part of living. We didn't squawk about it.

All the widows had serious physical infirmities and had lost beloved husbands many years before—but they all seemed immune to self-pity. One of the shaping experiences of their hardships was that they appreciated peace and prosperity more than those of us who take these things for granted.

We need to remember that our children are watching us and learning from us all the time, whether or not we're aware that we're teaching them.

CHAPTER 5

The Big Picture

To be alive, to be able to see, to walk, to have houses, music, paintings—it's all a miracle. I have adopted the technique of living from miracle to miracle.

ARTHUR RUBENSTEIN

Only a life in the service of others is worth living.

ALBERT EINSTEIN

Throughout history, people who are suffering have looked to a higher power for help and comfort. Polls conducted in the week after the September 11th attacks showed that 90 percent of Americans had at least one symptom of stress and 90 percent of these people "turned to religion" to help them cope.[1] Religion is *the* primary means of coping with stress for older Americans.[2]

Although almost all American adults profess a belief in God (poll results fall between 90 and 95 percent),[3] religion no longer holds the preeminent place in our society for children that it once did. Church and synagogue attendance has been steadily declining during the lifetime of the Millennial generation—only one out of every three American families attends religious services on a weekly basis. In 1981, an average American child between the ages of three and eleven spent nearly two hours a week in religious activity, such as going to church. By 1997, far fewer children attended services and the group average had dropped to slightly more than one hour a week.[4]

These statistics are significant because strong religious beliefs can help immunize both children and adults against stress. Although psychological research on the benefits of religion is scarce (psychologists as a group are much less religious than the general population[5]) the studies that do exist have found that most people (50 to 85 percent, depending on the study) say that they find religion helpful in tough times. These studies looked at combat veterans and at people who had lost a child, had cardiac or transplant surgery, had a physically handicapped child, were diagnosed with cancer, or had been the victims of abuse.[6]

Other studies have looked at more objective benefits (i.e., not just a person's opinion) of religion. Religious coping—such as church attendance, seeking spiritual support, interpreting the stress or trauma in a spiritual context (e.g., God's will), or being supported by a religious congregation—is demonstrably helpful for about four out of every ten persons. For example, in a study of 1,423 adult victims of drunk drivers, those who attended church most frequently *before* the crash were less likely to suffer the debilitating symptoms of PTSD afterward.[7]

A parent's religiosity also seems to have trickle-down

benefits for their children. Kids raised in religious families are, for example, less likely to use drugs and alcohol, or have behavior problems such as aggression. For adolescent girls, there is a lower risk of getting pregnant.[8]

There are sound psychological reasons that religion can help us during tough times—and, as parents, all of us can help immunize our children against stress by understanding its therapeutic aspects. Whether we're religious or not, we need to recognize the importance of belief systems, the benefits to our kids of rituals and communities, and the power that faith has to heal and soothe. We can help our children by teaching them that there is something larger than the self, and that meaning and purpose in life that can be found in a selfless dedication to others.

The Psychology of Religion

It is a fundamental human characteristic to try to understand our experiences, good or bad. We crave explanations. Eminent neurologist Michael Gazzaniga says that making order out of chaos—coming up with coherent explanations for what we see, hear and feel—is one of the things human brains do best. Gazzaniga believes that an "interpreter," located in the left cerebral cortex (in right-handed people), fits our experiences together into a coherent whole.[9]

Our need for explanations is so powerful that the interpreter instantly constructs a theory for any occurrence. Our minds are uncomfortable with a lack of meaning. We want all the pieces of the puzzle to fit together. According to Gazzaniga, religion attracts us because it gives us a ready-made set of explanations.

There is a special urgency, a greater need for understanding when our experience is stress-inducing or traumatic. We strive to uncover the cause of difficult events so we can avoid them in the future. Forewarned is forearmed! We seek the meaning of misfortune. What did we do to deserve this suffering? we ask ourselves. Is it karma? Fate?

During the black plague in Europe (1347–1350), one out of every three people perished. Many people sought an explanation for the devastation in the teachings of the church. Some clerics taught that, like Noah's proverbial flood, the plague was caused by man's sinfulness.[10]

In response to the plague, many people practiced intercessionary rituals, such as self-flagellation, hoping penance would appease an angry God. Going from town to town whipping oneself may not seem like an effective remedy for stress, but it was better than being baffled and doing nothing as a result. *Any* action that helps us cope with stress or trauma, when we believe that action will help relieve the cause of our suffering, will make us feel less helpless, less powerless.

———

According to Sigmund Freud, human vulnerability is the mother of religion. Freud wrote that belief in an almighty protector is an illusion—something that we wish were true but isn't. "We are helpless and afraid and look to replace the strong loving father of our infancy with God the father," Freud wrote in *The Future of an Illusion*. The vast power of the natural world (including its deadly microbes) and our struggle with ourselves—the impulses we have difficulty controlling—can be terrifying when viewed from the perspective of our relative powerlessness.[11]

I agree with Freud: Religion helps us deal with our feelings of helplessness; and the thought of an omnipotent God watching over us can be comforting. Freud, however, missed the most important stress-immunizing effect of religion: it can tell us what *action* to take when calamity befalls us, whether that action is to pray, to meditate on the illusionary nature of the self, or to do penance.

Ritual

Religious ritual is comforting. In Catholicism, there are nearly four thousand patron saints that one can appeal to in times of need. James the Greater, for example, is the patron saint of arthritis suffers, equestrians, and soldiers. As a somewhat absent-minded Catholic child, I remember praying to St. Anthony of Padua—the patron saint of lost articles—on the numerous occasions when I had lost my wallet, glasses, or a favorite toy.[12]

Florence, a seventy-two-year-old widow, describes how participating in the traditional Jewish ritual of mourning helped her cope with being alone after fifty-two years of marriage. "I went to *shul* every day and said *kaddish* for my husband. I think that the fact that I got up every day was beneficial for me. That means going to *shul* every day for eleven months. This forces you to go out and be with people, and I got a sense of serenity and understanding that this is life. I think religion was a major factor that helped me cope with the stress of loss, of being suddenly alone. It forced me to do something. I had to be in *shul* at 8:30, dressed and everything. While you say kaddish for the dead, it may be more beneficial for the living."

———————

When I was a psychological consultant to a Catholic prep school, I was called in to help kids on cases of suspected abuse, when they were in trouble academically, when they or their parents were suspected of substance abuse, when they exhibited suicidal tendencies, and when there had been a death in the school.

In one case, a head-on car crash into a tree had killed one of the students as well as boys from other schools. The story was all over the newspapers. After reading the story, some of my therapist friends called me to offer their sympathy and support. I remember one, in particular, saying, "You must be incredibly busy dealing with the accident." My reply surprised him. "No," I said. "Dealing with death is what Catholics do best."

In contrast to other events I had to deal with, for this tragedy, the coping strategies were well-defined. The rituals were all in place. The students gathered together in the church. There was a funeral mass. The priests talked about what the boy's death meant and what we, the living, should take from it. These coping strategies have been refined over the two-thousand-year history of Catholicism, and they are a comfort to many.

Ritual in and of itself can be a great comfort, but when it is combined with a belief in the importance and efficacy of the action, its power can be truly transformative.

Belief

According to the Bible, faith can move mountains. The literal interpretation of that New Testament passage (Matthew 17:20) may seem far-fetched to the modern American, but its essence is supported by a growing body of scientific research.

According to Dr. Jerome Frank, a noted psychiatrist and author of the classic study of psychotherapy *Persuasion and Healing*, belief can be vitally important in recovery from disease. Based on his study of healing practices across various cultures, Frank determined that two of the most important factors in whether a person benefits from treatment (whether it is $250 per hour Park Avenue psychoanalysis, a trip to the fountain at Lourdes, or a shaman's incantations) is that there is a "rationale, conceptual scheme or myth that provides a plausible explanation for the patient's symptoms and prescribes a ritual or a procedure for resolving them" and that the patient (and, optimally, the healer) believe that the explanation and ritual are correct.[13]

Even skeptics have a hard time discounting research on the placebo effect—how, for example, before the advent of modern medicine, patients were cured of illnesses with non-therapeutic drugs such as *usnea*, which was made from moss from the skulls of victims of violent death. In fact, it is not an exaggeration to state that the history of medicine before the modern period was primarily the history of the placebo effect.[14]

Research shows that placebos—sugar pills, usually—are effective in 24 to 58 percent of patients. Placebos are 59 percent as effective as anti-depressants (tricyclics), 58 percent as effective as non-drug treatments of insomnia, and 54 to 56 percent as effective as common painkillers, including injected morphine.[15]

The kind of belief that gives the placebo efficacy also applies to our children's behavior and their general sense of well-being. Children's success in school is tied to their expectations. If they believe that they can succeed, they often will. A teacher's belief in them will also improve their chances for success.

I worked once with an African-American boy who was attending a predominantly white school. I met with his mother to discuss his poor grades. She said that, in general, his teachers didn't expect much from him because he was black.

"He'll never do well until his teachers believe he can do the work," she said. "There's a kind of subtle prejudice working against him."

Studies of urban black children indicate that even though they begin their schooling with scholastic aptitude equal to whites, their lower achievement in the first year of school, considerably influenced by their teacher's expectations, sets the stage for an ever-widening difference in academic achievement that extends into high school.[16]

This kind of subtle prejudice works against many students—and, as we parents know, a teacher's preconceptions or prejudices are sometimes hard to break.

When children expect to be liked, they are more likely to be liked. Third graders were told either that some children they had met the week before had really liked them or were told nothing. When they were put together in a group again, the kids who were told that they were liked by the new kids were actually liked more than the kids in the control group.[17]

Placebos—both physical and psychological—work, especially for children, who are impressionable. Rather than bemoan the fact that belief is an important therapeutic ingredient, we, as parents, should embrace it.

Connection

While religious or spiritual feelings are an individual experience, organized religion is communal. When psychologists study the ways in which organized religion helps people in times of need, the social support provided by the group is vitally important. Religious communities provide a ready-made fund of social capital.

Even without a group, people who have a personal relationship with God or a higher power may feel a palpable presence that helps them feel less alone, less isolated. As a child, I was taught that I had a guardian angel who watched over me day and night. He was real to me. Some people have similar relationships with departed loved ones. They report being able to feel their presence. Sometimes they even see them.[18]

Florence recounts that when she was recently widowed, her dead husband appeared to her and got her out of bed one morning, so she could get to *shul* on time. "I actually felt him brushing my hand, saying 'Get up! Get up!' And I said, 'Okay! I'm going already!' But he wasn't there."

Something Larger than Ourselves

Albert Einstein didn't believe in a personal God but considered himself to be a deeply religious man. Einstein was awed by the mysterious. Staring into the sky at night, he would marvel at its immensity, its beauty, and the miracle that humans could comprehend some of its workings, however imperfectly.

In his book *The World As I See It*, Einstein wrote: "It was the experience of mystery—even if mixed with fear—that engendered religion. A knowledge of the existence of something we cannot penetrate, of the manifestations of the profoundest reason and the most radiant beauty, which are only accessible to our reason in their most elementary forms—it is this knowledge and this emotion that constitute the truly religious attitude; in this sense, and in this alone, I am a deeply religious man."[19]

All the religions with which I am familiar have, at their core, a giving over of oneself to God, a resignation, a selflessness. This submitting to something larger than ourselves is a fundamental part of twelve-step recovery programs, such as Alcoholics Anonymous. Steps two and three are ". . . Believe that a Power greater than ourselves could restore us to sanity and [make] a decision to turn our will and our lives over to the care of God as we [understand] Him."[20] It's important to remove oneself from the center of the things—to put God, country, or our fellow man first, to recognize our insignificance in the universe. It gives us perspective. We can see the big picture. It helps us not sweat the small stuff. Most importantly, from the perspective of stress immunization, it lessens fear.

This perspective made it possible for some soldiers to tolerate the stress of combat. George McGovern, the 1972 Democratic Party nominee for president and veteran bomber pilot who flew thirty-five combat missions,[21] told me that he found it easy to serve. "I learned that you are not the most important thing in the world," he said. "The world is. I never had had any question about fighting Hitler or what I did during the war."

It's important to give our children a sense of the importance of things outside themselves—and not just for moral reasons. It's not psychologically healthy to be self-centered.[22]

The less self-centered we are, the easier it will be for us to cope with stress. Anxiety cannot exist without self-focus. Take one of our most prominent fears: public speaking. Standing in front of an audience makes us anxious because we are afraid we are going to mess up, sound stupid, or be boring. We're completely exposed. There's no place for us to hide. It's like the dreams many of us periodically have where we're naked in public. It's an ego threat. By not measuring up to some self-set standard of competence, our view of ourselves is threatened. We become self-conscious, self-blaming, or self-pitying. Not focusing on the "self" minimizes the threat to our self-esteem.

How are we going to help our children learn this? And, barring combat experience, how does learning to be less self-centered carry over to situations when more than our self-esteem is at stake? One of the benefits of realizing we're not the center of the universe is our ability to be able to see the world from a perspective other than our own and to forgive—ourselves and others. It is important that we teach these traits to our children. In hard times, we want them to be able to treat other people with compassion, not to turn in on ourselves and become bitter and insular. Father Sean McManus is a model in this respect.

"The Troubles": Father Sean McManus

I am Irish on my father's side, the descendant of fishermen who eked out a living setting out from the northeastern coast into the gray-green Irish Sea. My father is proud of his heritage, and with his help I have visited our homeland on more than one occasion.

Like many Irish Americans, I have been troubled by the perpetual violence in Northern Ireland. While traveling there in the early 1980s, I saw BRITS OUT signs spray-painted across the North. As an American, it was hard for me to completely understand what made the problem so momentous. As a child, I wondered why Catholics and Protestants were killing each other in Belfast when on my suburban street in Wheaton, Illinois, Catholics and Protestants got along just fine.

"The Troubles"—a major escalation in violent confrontations, bombings, and unrest that began in 1968 and plagued Northern Ireland for 30 years—are finally over. Nevertheless, tension between Catholics and Protestants is still pronounced.[23]

———

Father Sean McManus, a Catholic priest, is the founder and president of the Irish National Caucus, a human rights lobby in Washington, D.C., that works for peace and justice in Northern Ireland. He says that he saw that the problems in Northern Ireland weren't going to be solved by the "triangle" of London, Belfast, and Dublin. "An outside entity was needed," McManus said. He wanted to muster the 40 million Irish Americans to put pressure on the British government to resolve the issue of English rule in Northern Ireland.

The caucus has helped bring about peace in Northern Ireland. "Today, we see more hope for a lasting resolution of the conflict than at any point during the last hundred years," he said. "But the hard-won peace is fragile."

McManus lost his brother to the Troubles. I wanted to see how he had managed to transcend that tragedy and to work in a positive, non-violent way for social justice. I went to see him in Washington, D.C. Broad-shouldered, garrulous, with a sonorous brogue, he wears his passion for the oppressed on his sleeve.

I asked him about his brother's death.

"Patrick was killed the very day my sister was married," McManus said. "The priest woke us up (the only time you saw a priest in those days was when someone had been killed) and he told us that the night before at 10:25 my brother had been killed. He was transporting a bomb to blow up a local British customs post. It went off when he was handing it to one of his fellows. It killed him and injured several other people."

"After you heard this news did you have feelings of hatred and revenge against the British and Protestants?"

"No. Never. My parents had instilled us with a proper Christian attitude. Most people still don't understand that it is the Republican tradition in Ireland to oppose unjust structures. When we liberate ourselves it is also the oppressors who are liberated. That philosophy and outlook was key to my family's survival. We were able to forgive, let go, and heal. Isn't this how forgiveness occurs? We forgive because God forgives us. That's the deal!"

"What did your brother's death do to your psychology as a child?"

"This may sound extraordinary. I was sixteen, and I had to make a decision. Did I join the IRA and fight for Ireland or did I dedicate myself to God and the priesthood? It may shock people, but they were two perfectly devout choices."

"You've done both, though."

"Thanks to God, that's the blessing I've been given. And I thank God that I was never involved in the violence because I've come to totally accept the philosophy of nonviolence. My brother's death probably traumatized all of us—well, I know it did. I dealt with it through the sheer fervor of religious devotion. It also gave me the sense of: 'My brother gave his life for a cause. Sean, you better shape up and seriously commit to something in your life with your whole self.'

Others, faced with similar circumstances, might go crazy or go to drugs. But in our family my mother was profoundly religious. She had invincible faith, and she was a very powerful person."

"Her faith got her through your brother's death?"

"Absolutely. And all my brothers and sisters would say exactly the same. I'll tell you what kind of person my mother was. There was an attempt to kill her (because another of her sons was an outspoken member of the British Parliament) by a local Protestant fellow, a fellow we knew all our lives. He shot upstairs into her bedroom. A couple of nights after the shooting, I was sitting with her in the kitchen and there was a knock on the door. I went out and there was one of the tallest policeman I've ever seen in my life, six foot seven. He said that the man who had shot at her was there to apologize to Mrs. McManus. [The man] said, 'I'm sorry, Mrs. McManus. Will you forgive me?' Without blinking an eyelid, she said, 'Of course I do, dear. God loves you!' And she grabbed his hand. I'll tell you the truth, I didn't feel like grabbing his hand. I felt more like taking his head off. But it was a graphic example of her forgiveness."

No family in Northern Ireland was untouched by the dread that they or someone they loved would become a victim of the Troubles. McManus coped by becoming a combination of his mother and his brother, Patrick, who served as a substitute for his aging father. He has his mother's deep religious faith, which has allowed him to take refuge in God and to forgive others their trespasses. He absorbed his brother's patriotic fervor and idealism. Patrick's death galvanized him. It pushed him to do something meaningful with his life—to commit to something bigger than himself.

They had to overcome the pain of Patrick's death. McManus said the family still cries over it, but they don't allow their sorrow to impede their moral sense that it is better to forgive than to seek vengeance or to harbor bitterness.

McManus's own ability to forgive exemplifies the attitude of people who have successfully recovered from trauma: He doesn't allow the past to dominate the present. He could have been haunted by his brother's death, but he wasn't. He could be walking around full of hatred for British rule. But he has lived his life.

In the final section of this chapter, I suggest practical ways to instill these values in our kids, but first a couple more examples of people who have been able to cope with stress by focusing on something larger than themselves.

Theresa Stichick, Refugee Worker

Theresa embodies the idea of giving back, of service, of helping others. She would periodically disappear from classes at the Harvard School of Public Health. Eventually, we grew accustomed to her sudden departures. "Oh, Theresa's probably just off somewhere saving the world," we'd say when she disappeared.

Theresa is the product of her environment. Her father was a Peace Corps volunteer in Africa. Her mother is a special education teacher. When they were first married, Theresa's parents moved to the interior of Alaska, which was where

Theresa was born. There the Stichick family continued to work helping people in need. Theresa caught the bug; while working toward her doctorate, she has volunteered in far-flung refugee camps, helping displaced children.

I met with Theresa in November 2001, when we were all still feeling the aftershock of 9/11. She provided inspiration for the kind of values most of us would like to instill in our kids.

"When I first started working with refugee kids in 1998, I spent a month in Albania," she said.[24] "I started up emergency education programs, usually at the request of community members, especially parents, who in this case are in large refugee camps in the Tiranë area. They came from Kosovo, fleeing from the fighting. The idea was to establish some kind of meaningful, structured, predictable activity in their lives. We had to think of education as something to restore meaning and predictability.

"We asked every kid, 'What are your hopes for the future?' 'For the war to end,' they say. 'For there to be peace.' 'To get a job.' 'To have a family.' 'To help rebuild my country.' And I'd see that the kids who seemed to be doing well [in the camps] were the kids who got engaged in something meaningful, even if it is caring for a sick elderly refugee. Kids are hungry for that. Give them a positive role. That little bit of meaning can save them.

"That's why the advice from the [Bush] administration after 9/11 to keep living your life is so bizarre. Back in the days of JFK it was, 'Ask not what your country can do for you, ask what you can do for your country.' I think people here were hungry for something to do, and so after the 9/11 attacks they ran to the blood donation centers and they sent money to the Red Cross. You've got to feed that sentiment or you miss an opportunity to help people recover. And just to tell people to go back to their materialistic, self-absorbed lives—buy stuff, go pamper yourself, go to a show—I think is a missed opportunity. I really think there is a lot that we don't tap into about people helping each other. It's beyond simply increasing social support. It's also about meaning and purpose and giving back to others."

Steve Ross: Coming of Age in the Camps

To my mind, there is no more graphic example of children's successful adaptation to stress than that of concentration camp survivors who have gone on to lead full lives. I have read the studies and been inspired. Many, according to Sarah Moskovitz's moving book *Love Despite Hate*, have not only survived, they have put hate, self-pity, and entitlement aside and "their lives are marked by an active compassion for others."[25]

To understand how this could occur, I wanted to talk to one of these child survivors face-to-face. I needed to know how someone who had experienced the most unhappy childhood imaginable, who had been the victim of unbounded hatred, could have any love left in his heart. In one of the many happy twists of fate that marked my research for this book, one day while waiting for a pizza, I saw an announcement that Steve Ross—concentration camp survivor and youth worker—would be speaking that week at a local school. He graciously agreed to meet with me—for three long sessions, as it turned out. I went to our first meeting carrying a tape recorder and a head full of questions about how giving back to others helped him recover from trauma.

Our interview took place at a school near the top of Boston's Mission Hill, home of a city program that reaches out to street kids. "I was involved with kids in the city for over forty years," said Steve, "and now they ask me to come back here. I'm retired, seventy years old. But I am involved with these kids, and I've learned a lot. I go to see them in jail, to make sure somebody is supporting them. I got them out of jail, and I was able to kick them back into school, or into jobs. I kissed people's asses so they would allow some of these kids into their system, into the network, so that they could be part of the establishment. It worked well."

How does Steve's past inform the work he does today? Steve's story of his experience in the camps is impossible to fully comprehend. When the Nazis began rounding up Jews in Poland, Steve's parents first tried to escape with their children into Russia. Many of the Jewish children who survived the Holocaust did so in Russian internment camps. But the border was closed to Steve's family. His parents knew their lives hung by a thread, and they sent Steve to live with a family deep in the country. The family taught him Catholic prayers and enough Polish (his family only spoke Yiddish) to "pass" as a non-Jew. To earn enough money to survive, he worked at a Nazi army base shining boots. But one day, a suspicious soldier took Steve's pants off. When they saw that he had been circumcised, he was sent to the camps in 1939, when he was only nine years old.

It is difficult to estimate how many children were sent to concentration camps, because the Nazis never registered many of them. Usually, they were the first ones killed because their ability to work was limited.

I asked Steve about his early family life to see if there were some clues there that would help explain why he survived when so many others perished.

"I was in ten camps. We ended up from Auschwitz at a little place called Beitinghardt. It was an empty camp, nothing there except barracks. They put seven or eight hundred people in a barrack fit for sixty. Lice crawled all over us. We slept close together, on bare boards with nothing to cover ourselves. I shivered all night, but somehow we slept. And, somehow, some of us survived."

"I think it's amazing to many of us who lived through it that you could survive."

"I know what human beings can endure," Steve replied. "I was about twelve when we arrived in Auschwitz. Women were putting blood on their cheeks to make them red so that they wouldn't be selected to die. People were losing their arms by machines and they were saying, 'Put on a tourniquet so you don't lose the blood.' And put whatever you have, a jacket, a shirt around the limb. And some people survived. There was no water. I didn't take a shower for five years. I never washed my face. I never saw any hot water. The skin on my body was broken up with scabies. You didn't have enough water to drink, let alone wash your face. I went to get a little water in my dish and I was sexually molested by the Ukrainian guards. Sexually molested. I'm not ashamed to tell you that."

"How was your stress level after the war?"

"Terrible. I would sit down and focus my eyes on one object. I'd sit like that for hours. I was seeing things—my mother going into the gas chamber. I saw that, and I was seeing it again. And then my mother was saying to my father, 'Yussel, didn't I tell you they were going to murder us. Well, they're going to murder us now.'"

"You saw your mother going into the gas chamber?"

"Yes. It was hard for me to trust after that. We robbed, stole from and betrayed one another in the camps. You saw people dying; you didn't even care. You knew you were next. It was such selfishness in all of us. You can't envision it. You can't really make sense of it, but that's the way it was. There are things too terrible to think of. The doctors who were with us told us not to move our bowels, because you dried up your intestines; there was nothing to put into your system. There wasn't even any water; we drank pee. We managed to live with this kind of stress, and this kind of anxiety, and we learned to survive. We had bloody feet, and we had no hope, but always there was somebody around you who said, 'You can't lose hope.' There was one man, a goldsmith, he liked me and adopted me, gave me a piece of bread occasionally. Each day in our barracks there were eighty to a hundred people dead. Some had committed suicide at night. Some had hanged themselves. Some had slit their throats with a piece of metal from a sardine can. You learned to live with stress. And today you're living in heaven, heaven. I have been deeply affected by the war. I still cry. Even today, and I am seventy years old."

"How have you gotten help?" I asked.

"I think that stress is very much helped if you have someone to talk to, if you have someone you love. My wife is a tremendous therapist. She listens and she says, 'How could you ever not be affected by some of these things?' And we talk about it. Her love and care for me, all the talking has helped me. The fact that I have a beautiful family. That I've been able to work. I work all the time. I need to keep busy. I've re-sided our house. And, you know, I believe in this country and our way of life."

"How did you feel after the attacks on the World Trade Center?"

"The planes crashing into the two towers—it bothers me, I want to tell you. My wife and I were sitting, crying, and we were talking about it. It bothers me terribly because this country does not deserve it. If you put all the other countries together they won't make what this country is all about. After the attacks, a billion dollars was raised for the Red Cross. People were giving whatever they had. They gave time, energy. The firemen, police, paramedics were Americans who died in defense of our country. You have to tell this to the kids. And you need to help them."

"You're one of those people. You help out kids."

"I go to the projects. I'm not scared to go into the worst areas of Boston. I have a place where I put all the weapons I find on these kids: knives, zip guns, brass knuckles. Do you know the talent that went into making some of these weapons? The kids talk to me. And by helping them, I have helped myself."

"It's amazing that you've managed to keep this connection to life."

"I have been able to expose my sensitivity and my affection to others. I have managed to bring my own two children up in such a way that they were always inquisitive and impressionable, and they always wanted to be cognizant of my growth and development. They always were questioning, inquisitive, about learning from me. I always loved and cared for them. I always treated them with compassion and affection and they picked up these traits from me."

"So they felt the love?"

"Yes. The love I got from my parents I've passed on to them. My parents were such loving people. They didn't have much, yet they gave us everything."

Before I left Steve, a boy, maybe seventeen years old, walked down the hall toward us. Steve smiled. It was the first real expression of joy I had seen from him. The boy was smiling, too. They hugged. Steve turned to me and said, "I want you to meet someone. When I first found him he had nothing. Now look at him. He is a wonderful boy." He then turned to the boy and playfully demanded, "Open your mouth." The boy complied. A large silver stud was anchored in his tongue. Steve looked back at me. "When I first met him, he had, can you imagine, three piercings in his tongue. Three!" He looked back at the boy. There was mischief in his eyes, and love, too—warm paternal love. "I got rid of the first two and I am going to get rid of that one, too. You'll see."

What can today's parents take away from Steve's remarkable story? At the very least, inspiration and hope—the knowledge that no matter how bad things get for a child, recovery is possible. Beyond that, I hope Steve's story illustrates the healing power of giving to others. At one level, Steve is saving himself when he pulls a child off the street or out of jail and gets him into school or helps him land a job. He is liberating himself from the camps. In less dramatic fashion our children will cope better with their own stress when they too are focused on others. In the research for my last book, *Too Much of a Good Thing*, I found that community service—getting out and helping to feed homeless people or helping to clean litter from public places—helps teens avoid problems such as drug use, depression, permissive sexual attitudes, and eating disorders. Children who helped others with their problems had fewer of their own. It gave meaning to their lives, a better view of the all-important Big Picture.

Summing Up—Helping Your Children

Religion, broadly construed, is an effective way of coping with stress for many people. It doesn't help everyone, and in some cases it can be detrimental, as when, for example, guilt and fear are magnified because a stress or trauma is seen as a punishment sent by God. It brings comfort and courage when one or more of the following therapeutic components comes into play: an overarching worldview or belief system, faith, ritual, connection to others, and recognition that there is something more important or "bigger" than self. Parents can use these aspects of religion as a guide in their efforts to immunize their children against stress.

Belief System

Children, especially younger ones, endlessly ask "why?" It is our job to give them answers, to give their left forebrain "interpreter" some concepts to work with. Our job is made easier if we use a ready-made belief system such as those found in organized religions. What happens to people when they die, a child asks? Answers to these tough existential questions are given in the Bible, the Koran, or the sutras.

If we're not committed to an organized religious tradition, it's important to come up with a substitute belief system that provides some answers to big questions. If we're unsure what to say, we need to do some self-exploration to try to figure out what our own beliefs are. Then we need to communicate them to our child in an age-appropriate way. We don't need to go into great detail or give more information than our children request. I can't tell you what to believe, although I can tell you that it is good for your child if you help him find the answers.

Secular parents who choose not to give their child the structure of a religious tradition should try to find a "big thing" to replace it. This might be a philosophy or a family credo, and it should be something that will fill some of the same psychological needs as religious faith. It must be something transcendent, some idea or purpose that goes beyond the needs of the individual.

History and philosophy can help the secular parent here. Socrates, for example, focused on two big ideas: Truth and Beauty. Freud believed in the god *logos*, which in its essence is reason or science, the search for truth with rational thought. Einstein, as we saw earlier, found his god in the mysteries of the universe and our attempts to understand them. To this he added service to others.

Religious traditions often include a set of ideals or laws that are meant as a guide to life—the Ten Commandments, the Noble Eightfold Path of Buddhism, or simply the Golden Rule. These may be adopted or adapted by a parent and taught to the child as a big idea, a higher purpose, a way of living that puts others above self.

This big thing may well overlap with whatever belief system one imparts to a child. If, like Freud, a parent is devoted to *logos*, the answers to some of the existential questions will follow. Questions about death could, for example, be answered with a circle-of-life metaphor. It will be best, as I discussed in the section on social referencing, if a parent doesn't convey his or her anxiety about these questions to a child. They will draw their emotional cues from you.

A parent can also provide focus by her own involvement in a wider community and by pointing out that there are always those who are less fortunate than ourselves and need our attention. Thus a child can, at least be made aware that she or he is not alone with hardship and that other people have needs as well.

Selflessness carries with it an ability to forgive. Secular parents may wonder how they can translate the Christian message of forgiveness into their homes. How can we help our children have compassion for people who do hurtful things to us and to others? Parents ask me all the time how they should respond if their kids are being bullied in school.

Help your kids consider where the bullying comes from, I say. Ask them to think about why someone would take pleasure from their pain. What does that say about that person's life? How bad does their life have to be that they want to pass on their pain? We can raise our children to try to understand that a bully may himself have been bullied; someone who teases may feel bad about himself—inferior in some way. One of the reasons that the WTC was attacked is because so many of the attackers and the people in the societies they come from lead hopeless lives. They pass their pain on to us.

The passing around of pain is the same dynamic of hopelessness that works in families: the abused becomes the abuser, the outcast becomes the tormentor. Now that we are a world community we can't afford to dismiss the suffering of far-flung people as having nothing to do with us. We can meet aggression with aggression. Or we can choose to break the cycle. We can teach our kids to follow the example of Father McManus (who took his inspiration from Martin Luther King and Mahatma Gandhi). We can help them say: The pain stops here. We can teach our children to act as a positive force in the world, in the way that Theresa has, as a volunteer relief worker with kids in refugee camps. If they act in this way, they, like Steve Ross, will give as well as receive.

Ritual and Faith

Designing rituals for children when they are under stress will give them something to hold on to, and, more importantly, something to believe in. Earlier I talked about the dream catcher or bad dream eliminator. The child places his faith in an object that his parent has empowered, and he is soothed. Many parents instinctively develop rituals for when a child has physical pain—kiss it where it hurts, a special Band-Aid or salve—but we tend to be less resourceful when it comes to psychological pain.

Some examples you may find helpful: When a child has lost something cherished, you can hold letting-go ceremonies. When you sense that the time is right, when it is time to let go, you can light a candle and talk about your child's happy memories of the person, animal, or thing that has been lost. Then you say that the candle's light symbolizes the memories you will carry inside your heart, but that when you blow it out you will let what's been lost go and move on.

You can also adapt religious rituals to your own purposes. Think about constructing a ritual for your child when he or she is upset. You might say: "When I'm upset, the first thing I do is go for a walk and try to appreciate all the beauty I see around me. That helps me put the problem in perspective. Then I think about all the things I am thankful for—like my family, my home, that I am loved [it's good to be specific here]. Once I have a little perspective on the problem, I start to really think about what the problem really is and what I can do about it."

Any child can benefit from a problem-solving ritual that approximates the scientific method. The first step is to specifically define the problem. If a child is afraid of a neighbor's dog, try to get him to figure out what it is about the dog that scares him. Is it a fear of being bitten? Of being barked at? If a child is afraid to sleep alone, is he afraid that someone will climb in the window or that there's a monster under the bed? The more specifically the problem can be defined, the easier it is to generate solutions.

Once the problem is defined, you and your child can generate solutions, then evaluate them. If you try something and it doesn't work, go back to the drawing board. The underlying rationale for this approach is that it teaches the child that she isn't powerless—that she has some measure of control over her life.

Drawing Strength from Others

As we saw in Chapter Three, religion often helps people cope with stress by providing a supportive community of people. Psychologists who study religious coping often point to "congregational support" as the most effective medicine in the church pharmacy.[26]

In Buddhist philosophy there are three refuges from life's suffering, one of which is the *sangha*—the community of believers. The decline of attendance at religious services that has occurred during the Millennial generation's lifetime is only one aspect of a wider erosion of community and social capital in America. As parents we need to make sure our children are well-connected, that they feel the support of a loving family, one that goes beyond the walls of our homes.

CHAPTER 6

————

Moving On

MACBETH: Canst thou not minister to a mind diseased,
Pluck from memory a rooted sorrow,
Raze out the written troubles of the brain . . . ?

DOCTOR: Therein the patient
Must minister to himself.

SHAKESPEARE, Macbeth, V. iii.

Echoes from the Past

Steve Ross, Holocaust survivor, suffers from PTSD. He can't rid himself of the memory of the unspeakable sights, sounds and smells of concentration camps where he was interned as a child. "I hear echoes," he says, a far-off look in his eyes, when he describes the way his Holocaust experiences have stayed with him. These echoes still come to him across the space of sixty years, often at night.

Steve told me about a dream that he'd had. "My mother put out two boxes with two geese. You could see the neck of one goose but the other had died. Nobody had fed the goose that was still alive. It was starving and dying of thirst. I was so angry that nobody was feeding it. It was so weak that it couldn't even make a noise anymore. I picked up the box and started shaking it. I could feel that there was a dead bird in there. I couldn't open it up. It was like the camps. You wanted to run away, but you couldn't.

"I tried to give the goose water, but something held me back. There were some kids in the dream, working in a kitchen—maybe like the one I had worked in at one of the camps, where we had to peel potatoes all day. If you ate one of those potatoes, the Nazis would kill you. I got caught once and they beat me. The kids in the dream were trying to get water. It wouldn't come out. I said, 'There's some dishwater. It's not bad. It looks okay. So let's give it to the goose. The goose drank it down so fast! I went to get more water, and then I woke up. I often have these dreams. Sometimes, I sweat. I can't get out of the dream, and I struggle."

We can see from this dream that even today Steve's early trauma is indelibly etched in his brain, just as we can see that he has been able to get on with his life. He is a devoted husband and father, and he does productive work with Boston's underprivileged kids.

One of the reasons Steve so impressed me is that he's led such a rich and meaningful life despite his early trauma. He has important lessons to teach all of us about how to move on from trauma and stress—lessons that are important for our children.

Steve has been able to move on by finding ways to cope with his painful memories. Contrary to popular psychological wisdom, he's done this, in part, by *avoiding* these memories, rather than exhuming and examining them.

"I've been able to live with stress and cope because I'm always busy," he said. "When I'm not reading or writing, I work with my hands. I have shingled our house. I took the walls out. I made it like the 1800s. I work hard all the time."

Steve's adaptation is extreme because his memories are intense. But suppression is not necessarily a bad thing. It can be an important part of a healthy coping strategy, a way of getting the space necessary from painful memories to be able to reconstruct our lives.

Let's examine how stress works on our memories, conditioning us to reexperience traumas, reacting in automatic and often counterproductive ways long after the triggering event or events have passed.

Stress, Trauma, and Memory

PTSD is, in important ways, a memory disorder.[1] People with PTSD, like Steve, suffer from hypermnesia—vivid, disturbing memories that they can't keep at bay. Paradoxically, amnesia— where a traumatic event is forgotten or repressed—is also part of this syndrome. Car accident victims, for example, often don't remember anything that happened during the crash as well as in the minutes or hours just before or after it. But the residue of the experience remains. The memories are stored and often exert their influence unconsciously.

Scientists know this in part from a phenomenon known as "anniversary reactions." There is a case, famous among psychologists, of a woman who had survived a horrendous nightclub fire that occurred in Boston on November 28, 1942. Most of the patrons in the crowded club were unable to leave because the exits were blocked. Over four hundred people were killed, most from smoke inhalation. The woman had complete amnesia for the event—no recollection of even being in the building. Yet every November 28th thereafter, she reenacted her experience at the club—pulling fire alarms, trying to get people to evacuate whatever building she was in, fighting to escape from a fire that only burned in her memory.[2]

Less dramatic cases are also common. My wife has had the experience of finding herself uncharacteristically depressed. She searches for a reason, but comes up blank. The depression has apparently come to her out of the blue. Then it hits her. It's the anniversary of our child's stillbirth, her brother's fatal car crash, or her father's death. She is reliving the emotions of one of those dark days.

There are other examples of unconscious memories at work. Clinicians who work with abused children often find, for example, that the children have painful symptoms in bodily areas that were involved in the abuse even when there are no physical causes for them and they have no conscious recollection of the abuse.

The memory disorders associated with trauma are often severe. Nevertheless, we can learn from these extremes. They help us understand the principles that operate in children coping with less extreme forms of stress, because, in the final analysis, coping requires confronting memories.

Part of what we need to teach our children is how to move on after they've experienced a significant stress or trauma, how to keep painful memories from exerting too much influence over their lives. Understanding the ways these traumatic memories form and are modified by different kinds of coping strategies can help parents immunize their children against stress.

Emotional Memory

There are different types of memory. Two of the most important are *semantic memory* (sometimes called declarative) and *episodic memory* (sometimes called nondeclarative). Semantic memory is where facts are stored (the capital of North Dakota is Bismarck), as well as the conscious awareness of events that have happened (I was married in Memorial Church in Harvard Yard on September 14, 1985, on a warm day). In contrast (and most importantly for our purposes), episodic memories are emotional—the memory of how you felt when your child was born, or the fear you feel when you see a snake.

Trauma leaves strong traces in episodic memory. Flashbacks tend to flood people with powerful feelings. When Steve dreams about the starving goose, he has intense feelings, some of the same fear, anger, and sadness he felt in the camps. Nontraumatic, garden-variety stress also leaves an emotional memory trace, albeit a weaker one.

I remember a client with potent emotional memories that

I saw many years ago, a boy I'll call Dennis, who was just entering high school. Dennis was very bright, but extremely anxious. He lived his life in dread of ridicule and criticism. He was a talented writer, but he was afraid to show his work to others. He was too scared to order a pizza over the phone because he thought that he would be laughed at. Today, Dennis would probably be diagnosed as having social phobia and possibly treated with medication in conjunction with psychotherapy.

Treating Dennis was difficult because he didn't volunteer much information. I asked him what his earliest memory was. Most people can remember almost nothing that occurred before they were five years old. Dennis was no different. He described a scene in kindergarten when a teacher had chastised him for doing a drawing in black crayon. He remembered the shame he felt.

Dennis told me he had been the shortest child in the class and was unable to reach any of the other crayons that were stored on a shelf. Buoyed by his relative loquaciousness, I asked him about other early memories. They all had a similar ring—a scolding, a failure, an inability to live up to expectations. There were no good memories in the lot. They were all tinged with negative emotion, a subtle reexperiencing of the uncomfortable feelings associated with each incident, as if to remind him of the dangers inherent in social interaction.

Trace Memories

How did these negative memories get stored in Dennis's brain, and why did they have such a profound effect on his subsequent behavior?

Neuroscientists know that the brains of mammals are designed to remember emotionally significant material, events, and sensations that are relevant to our survival. An animal would, for example, be more likely to survive if he could remember where he had seen predators in the past. If a baboon was frightened by a cheetah near a watering hole at sundown, it would be advantageous for him to recall that event if he was ever near that same watering hole at twilight.

We are preprogrammed to remember some events more vividly than others. A prime example is our memory of food or drink that we think has made us ill. Eating edible, non-poisonous food is important for survival. Humans and other mammals are preprogrammed to vividly remember foods that have made them sick. This was ingeniously demonstrated in a study of children receiving radiation treatment for cancer. The children were given a new flavor of ice cream to eat just before they received the radiation. Shortly after receiving the radiation therapy, they had the characteristic reaction of feeling nauseous. The new ice cream flavor also became associated with the nausea, and the children came to detest it, even though they knew that it was the radiation that had caused the nausea.[3]

We tend to have strong memories of disturbing, frightening, or dangerous events. Ask almost any American over the age of fifty where he was when he heard that President Kennedy had been assassinated and he'll be able to tell you, usually in great detail. The current generation of children will have the same experience with 9/11. In previous chapters, we heard Prudence tell us that she remembers her father's death "like it was yesterday." Similarly Marion, though she was only six years old at the time, vividly recalls her sensations during her father's funeral.

Roughly speaking, the more emotionally intense an event is, the stronger its trace in memory. The primary stress hormone involved in emotional memory appears to be norepinephrine, the flight-or-fight hormone that raises our heart rate and energizes us for action—what, in more colloquial terms, we often call an adrenaline rush. Generally speaking, the more norepinephrine present, the stronger the trace.[4]

Opioids

Why, then, do trauma victims often have amnesia?

During extremely stressful situations, especially those that involve physical pain, our bodies release pain-killing opioids. This helps us to focus on dealing with the situation rather than being overwhelmed by pain. The opioids allow an animal being attacked by a predator to concentrate on escape or defense. Opioids may be released for an extended time after extreme stress.

These endogenous opioids appear to interfere with memory—obscuring stressful events. Oxytocin, a hormone that produces contractions during labor, seems to have a similar memory-inhibiting function. This gives credence to the saying that if women really remembered the pain of childbirth, every child would be an only child. [5]

The Power of Memory

It isn't only bad memories that haunt us. Good ones do, too. When one is in the throes of romantic love, thoughts of a lover may be all-consuming. Children, especially young ones, can become obsessed with a toy they saw in a TV ad. Intense, pleasurable memories are at the root of addictions. A heroin addict doesn't start using heroin after being clean for six months because he is having withdrawal-induced stomach cramps. His craving stems from the intense memory of the pleasure the drug gave him. He can't get it out of his head.[6]

Part of the problem for the toy-fixated child, forlorn lover, or drug addict is that almost everything they see reminds them of their obsession. People who have had powerful emotional experiences tend to "remember" these events (with their accompanying emotions) all too easily.

When our rabbit, Rainbow, died a few years ago, my older daughter was saddened each morning when she woke up because her bedroom window looked out at the cage Rainbow had once occupied. It was a constant reminder of the loss, and Diana's days too often started on a note of sadness. Similarly, for people who were traumatized by the World Trade Center attacks, living or working near Ground Zero will bring forth continual emotional reactions. As a rule, the stronger the memory, the more likely it will return, brought to mind by even faint reminders.

Temperament

Why it is that two people can experience the same negative event and one's emotional memory is much stronger than the other's? Children come into the world with different temperaments—some cry at the slightest upset, others are placid amid adversity. When they get older, some are timid, others bold. Each child's personality—including the strength and character of his emotional memories—is always a blend of his genetic predispositions and life experiences.

An important part of a child's temperament has to do with the balance between seeking pleasure and avoiding pain. A parent can get a sense of this when she takes her child to an amusement park. When the child spies the roller coaster, does she pull her mom toward the ticket line in wide-eyed excitement or does she shrink back?

For the bold child, the anticipation of an exciting ride exerts a strong pull, while the internal voice that warns, "This could be scary and dangerous," is but a faint whisper. For the timid child, that same cautionary voice is loud and clear. The roller coaster may exert some draw, but the predisposition to avoid pain and danger exerts a strong influence.

A colleague, Enrico Mezzacappa, and I studied these temperamental differences in preteens. We used a kind of rigged slot machine.[7] We would give each of the children a dollar (ten dimes) and let them bet on the game a dime at a time. We told them they could play as long as they liked, providing they still had money. But we also clearly emphasized that they could stop playing at any time. The game was rigged so that the children won a dime on nine of the first ten plays, eight of the next ten, and so on. If they played 100 times, they would lose all the money we had given them. The average child would stop when he started to lose more than win, after sixty or seventy plays. Children who were very punishment-sensitive would stop much earlier, sometimes after their first loss. When we used this game at a school for behaviorally disordered children, most of whom had problems with impulse control, nearly all these kids played until their money was gone, at which point they invariably said, "I should have stopped when I still had money." For these children, the reward of winning was so salient that the "punishment" of losing had virtually no impact on their behavior.

Most children fall into a wide middle ground, neither reckless nor overly timid. But the parent who has a child at one of the extremes needs to take the child's temperament into account. A reason Dennis only remembered the bad times—the criticism and not the praise—was due, in part, to temperament. He was far more sensitive to punishment than reward.

As I'll discuss in a moment, Dennis's parents and I worked hard to help him get control over his painful memories—they were causing him too many problems. A parent of a bold or reckless child will have the opposite problem—they will need to try to get their child to recall dangers, drawbacks, and downsides, to make the voice of reason, caution, and conscience a little louder. To a bold six-year-old climbing a tree, a parent might have to say "Remember when you tried that last time and you fell and hurt yourself?"

I was asked once to be that voice for my eldest daughter, who, one night at 10:00, realized that she had procrastinated. Now that she could barely keep her eyes open, there was no way she could get all her homework done. "Dad, promise you'll remind me to do my homework as soon as I get home from school from now on," she begged.

Plucking from Memory a Rooted Sorrow

We need to help the sensitive child, whose negative emotional memories are intense and easily remembered, to forget. They will need help to come to terms with the past and move on. One of the keys to helping a child deal with stress is to lessen a painful memory's emotional weight.

Altering a painful memory—or in Shakespeare's eloquent phrase, plucking from memory a rooted sorrow—is not always straightforward, nor can it always be accomplished by a parent alone. Certainly in cases where the stress has been extreme or traumatic, a parent shouldn't hesitate to contact a psychologist or psychiatrist.

This said, there is much a parent can and should do (either alone or in conjunction with professional treatment) to help children deal with painful memories and, more importantly, to teach them the skills they'll need to deal with emotional memories when they are adults.

We can get a general guideline for how to help our children from clinicians who work with stress trauma or bereavement.[8]

There are three necessary steps in healing.

The first step is to come to terms with what happened, to have an explanation for the event that a child can tolerate— something that makes sense to them at an age-appropriate level. So, for a child who has lost a grandfather, the explanation might be that Granddad was old and people die when they get old. Moreover, the explanation may include some description of what happens after people die—"He's in heaven with Grandma." We've discussed why religious beliefs or other "big ideas" are so important: They make sense of difficult or mysterious events. Events for which the child has no explanation are more likely to bother him. They remain as "unfinished business," which begs to be put to rest.

The second step in healing involves working through the emotions associated with the event. "Working through" is a general term for, at a minimum, clarifying which emotions are involved (Does the child recognize that they feel sad, or is anger also present?), understanding what caused these emotions (Is the child afraid of the dark, what they imagine is in the dark, or of being alone?), and developing a greater level of comfort—less emotion—in thinking about the stressful events.

The third step is to move on—to reconstruct our lives and to live in the present, looking toward the future without being trapped by the past. This healing process involves creating new memories that are not as emotionally difficult. Therapists try to have their clients revisit and relive the event as they have remembered it, then work with them to lessen their fear or despair and to gain a new, less debilitating understanding of the event, so that they can move on with their lives.

Step 1—Understanding the Event at a Developmentally Appropriate Level

Therapists who work with trauma victims often find that the understanding of why these events occurred and hence the memories of the events are distorted. This is especially true of children, who tend to mix fantasy and reality and are egocentric—likely to see themselves as the cause of the traumatic event. The most commonplace example of this involves kids who really do believe that they are the cause of their parents' divorce. They may also have other unrealistic fears, such as being abandoned, unloved, or replaced. Thus, the task facing a parent is to get the child to accurately understand what has happened, to give them a reason that they can understand.

It is easy for adults to forget that children's explanations for why an event occurred will be childlike—naïve, unsophisticated—and that they will use only the limited range of concepts available to them. I once asked a five-year-old Julia when she was eating Swedish Fish candy, why she thought they were called *Swedish* fish.

She looked at me as though I was dense. "Because they're sweet!" she said.

———————

Only by creating an environment that welcomes open discussion can a parent find out what concepts and explanations a child is using to understand the stresses and strain in his life. This openness is one of the best ways to immunize a child against future stress. It means making time and really listening, not dispensing advice, judging, or steering the conversation in the direction you'd like it to go, but helping the child get the story out. This may involve open-ended questions (I don't quite understand what you mean, can you tell me more?) and reflecting back the content of what is said (it sounds like you were really scared when you heard that Grandpa died).

Once you have a sense of your child's understanding of the event, you can provide an explanation. I wouldn't hesitate to provide concrete answers or explanations even if you are unsure about whether they're correct. As a general rule, it is more important to be completely clear than completely right. Also, don't hesitate to be comforting, optimistic, or upbeat, even if deep down you feel uncomfortable, pessimistic, or downcast. The overarching principle behind all of the steps in healing is to give your child a sense that she has some control over her feelings and memories, and the events that caused them. Give her hope. Don't paint an unnecessarily bleak picture. Don't say, "Look, kid, these things just happen. Life is nasty, brutish, meaningless, and short—get used to it." Put a positive spin on it: "Sometimes bad things happen that make us sad. We don't even always know why. But in my experience the good and the bad tend to balance out over time."

Finally, make sure your child has understood your explanation. Ask him to tell you in his own words why he thinks the event happened. If he still has misconceptions, try explaining the event in a different way. This may take a while, but, in the end, your child will thank you.

Step 2—Working Through Emotional Memories

Back to Dennis. One of his salient memories was being scolded by a teacher in first grade. He told me that she hated him and had singled him out as a problem. This interpretation of the event had become habitual for him. It colored his reactions to other situations with teachers and classmates. He often felt criticized.

Part of the therapy I gave him involved analyzing the accuracy of his interpretation and correcting its flaws (especially given the fact that he could look at the event as a fourteen-year-old rather than a six-year-old). Through reflection, he came to see that it really was unlikely that she had hated him, and that if she did have strong feelings about him, then the problem was hers, not his. He knew that he had been a well-behaved and intelligent first grader.

This is just a snapshot of my work with Dennis, but it illustrates a technique that parents can use with their children. After you have found out how your child actually views the event, what his interpretation is, then challenge his false, irrational, or pathological assumptions.

Your job is to contrast reality with your child's distorted view of events. When a child whose parents are getting divorced says (as so many children do), "This will mess my life up forever!"—challenge that. This will involve figuring out what else he means. Does he mean: "I'll never have fun again"; or, "I'll always feel weird about this"; or, "Things will continue to get worse"? You can answer that, yes, the family will never be quite the same, but the other assumptions are false.

Using the example of other people, especially your child's peers who have gone through similar situations, can help dispel false assumptions. You can say, "Carol's parents were divorced last year and she seems okay about it now. Do you think that you might eventually end up like her?"

Some of the therapeutic magic of a support group (e.g. children of alcoholics, lupus sufferers) is that new members encounter people with problems similar to their own who have coped well. This concrete evidence of successful coping challenges a child's pessimism and brings with it realistic hope.

A similar technique was used in a therapeutic group for children who had lost a loved one—most commonly their father—in the crash of USAir Flight 427 near Pittsburgh in 1994. One of the early exercises the therapists used with the children was to have them each draw a picture of a happy event that had happened since the disaster. They used these pictures to challenge the children's often unspoken assumption that they would never be happy again.

The therapists in the Flight 427 group also had the children write letters to the deceased, to say things they wished they could have said but didn't. Bringing up this painful material in a supportive setting usually increased the child's tolerance of the bad feelings, and, over time, the repeated exposure to these thoughts minimized their impact.

The children were told that the letters could be a chance to settle "unfinished business." The therapists also used them to correct any false assumptions such as, "I should have warned my dad before he got on the plane." The purpose of the letter writing also involved an element of control or mastery. That is, even though the child could never actually say to the departed parent what they wanted to before the disaster, they can *do* something now: write the letter, say something similar to the surviving parent, fulfill an imagined wish of the deceased, be more supportive of a younger sibling, work harder in school, plant a tree in their memory.

Another important aspect of "working through" painful memories is to become conscious of when and how often painful thoughts occur, so that something can be done about them if they are too debilitating. Sometimes if the thoughts interfere with school or sleep or are just too painful, the child can be taught to control, stop, or replace them. By openly discussing with your child what kinds of thoughts she is having about the event, you can help her devise ways of controlling these feelings. If a child frequently is intruded upon by a disturbing image of a parent's funeral, they can be encouraged to consciously replace that image with one of the father's soul going to heaven or of a pleasant memory of their dad, or to simply shift attention outside their head to whatever is in their environment. Kids can be encouraged to use real or remembered objects, such as pictures or toys, to help them recall happy thoughts when upsetting ones are interfering with their lives. Practicing thought stopping or thought replacement can give children a greater sense of control over their emotions.

Active suppression of painful thoughts may have drawbacks. If it becomes habitual, it may promote pathological avoidance and anxiety. This is one of the reasons that it is recommended that children be told that these techniques are best used when the painful thoughts are interfering with important tasks such as school (you can even recommend that they replace the painful thought with, "I'll think about that later when I'm not so busy." Nevertheless, the simple concept that thought control is possible can be helpful and often goes unrecognized. Knowing that this control exists can be very empowering for a child.

Step 3—Moving On

After helping a child work through emotionally laden memories, we can help a child to move on—to come to see the stressful event relegated to the past. The therapists treating the kids of the Flight 427 victims, for example, had them create a story about themselves growing up, having a career and families of their own. This focused the kids on the future.

I'm afraid psychology hasn't always helped people move on. My sense is that today's parents are so concerned with how a child is feeling that they don't let them *forget*. We have become too worried about the perils of denial and forgotten the value of suppression.

Many of the people I interviewed about the traumas of the past—whether the Depression, World War II, or the flu pandemic—talked about the value of letting go and not dwelling on the past. Prudence Paine, the little girl who lived through her father's death and the Blitz, remembers a strong sense among the wartime British of this moving-on spirit.

"I think that we psychologize too much now," she said. "I do it, too. 'What's she feeling?' we say. 'We must do this or that for her.' Much of the time what we need to do is just get on with it. It's amazing what people can live through—concentration camps, for example. Look at what people are living through today. Think of what the Afghanis have had to deal with: It makes you want to weep.

"I think we all had the feeling [in wartime England]—a feeling that is missing sometimes in families now—that this is what we had to do. There's hardship and sorrow and then you get on with it. You get on with your life. Do you know what I'm trying to say?"

I agree with Prudence's impatience with the endless psychologizing and deification of feeling that we're prone to today. Psychologists have turned the pat phrase "How did you feel about that?" into a mantra to be silently repeated to oneself continually throughout the day. Of course, I don't believe we should deny significant feelings, but there is an important distinction between denial and suppression—the conscious decision to try to avoid painful feelings. The former is maladaptive, but the latter is adaptive—one gains control over the feelings rather than being controlled by them. This distinction is too often blurred.

It All Depends on How You Look at It

An important part of what makes an event stressful or traumatic is how threatened or helpless the child feels when it happens. As we discussed, children, especially younger ones, take their cues on how afraid they should be from their parents. But, as children get older, or when they experience stress when they're not in the company of a parent, they base how helpless they feel not only on how bad the event is, but also on their perception of their resources for dealing with it. One of the most important skills a parent can pass on to a child is the sense that they are never completely helpless.

We can draw inspiration from George McGovern's father. "When the bank failed," McGovern said, "we lost six thousand dollars. All the money we had. And I remember my dad saying, 'It's only money. We've got our health. We'll manage.' I never felt poor or deprived. None of us complained. Our parents told us what the financial situation was, and we lived with that. We rented out parts of the house to make money. My mother sewed clothes. I wore hand-me-downs.

The Depression was a great leveler. Everybody was in the same boat."

"It sounds as though your father set a great example for dealing with adversity," I said. "His reaction to losing everything is impressive."

"My father always quoted from the Bible that things work out best. I heard that all the time. That if one stood the course one could get through just about anything and that it might work out for the best. And I found that to be true in my life. I have lost several elections, but each time this has opened me up to new opportunities."

There are many possible ways to look at losing your life's savings—we're ruined, God is punishing us, everything is hopeless. Those feelings of helplessness make the event that much more stressful than it needs to be. It's important that we model resilience, fortitude, and optimism for our kids.

Every Survival Kit Should Include a Sense of Humor

I recently met Jothy Rosenberg when we featured speakers at a workshop for tenth-grade boys at a local public school. I was slated to talk about emotional development. Jothy, a successful businessman, was asked to talk to the boys about some of the adversity he encountered when he was in high school, over thirty years ago.

Jothy had been an accomplished athlete, competing in ice hockey and swimming. He was also an accomplished skier. But early in his sophomore year, Jothy started to feel pain in his right knee when he worked out. One day, after jumping rope, he asked his surgeon father to take a look at it. After a quick examination, his dad told him: "Big guys have knee pain." But the pain persisted. In fact, it got worse. His father finally took him to the hospital to have the knee thoroughly checked. Bad news. Cancer. The doctors told him that they had to amputate the next morning.

Today, Jothy is still an avid skier and he swims competitively. Although he's had to give up ice hockey, he's taken up long-distance biking. He still jumps rope, forwards and backwards—I've seen him. In the three decades since the amputation, he's obtained a Ph.D. in engineering. He's currently the CEO of a successful software company, married, with two children. He has also lost a lung (the cancer metastasized when he was in his early twenties).

When I asked him about how he managed to cope with his losses, and especially how his parents had helped him, Jothy paused. Then, from behind the big desk in his office, he told me: "They knew how to strike the right balance between supporting me and challenging me. It must have been hard as hell for my mom to watch me try to learn to ski again. The first time I got back on the slopes, I must have fallen 100 times while she watched. But I said, 'I can do this,' and they didn't try to stop me."

Jothy repositions his artificial leg and continues. "After I got out of the hospital, they bought a tractor and told me I still had to cut the grass."

An important way his parents helped Jothy cope was through humor. Soon after the operation, the family took a vacation. "We drove cross country in one of those monstrous

LTD station wagons," Jothy said. "We noticed that every time someone passed us they were staring at the car. We thought one of the tires was low. We stopped but couldn't see anything wrong. Then my mom figured out that everybody must have been looking at my artificial leg, which was stored in the back of the station wagon. They were trying to figure out where the body was. We had a good laugh. And after that we did all sorts of things with the leg—like sticking it out the car window!"

Jothy has maintained his sense of humor. "I was biking the other day," he said, "and some guy backed out of a parking space too quickly. I almost got around him but he knocked me over. The guy hopped out of his car, worried that he might have killed me. You should have seen the look on his face! There I am lying on the ground underneath my bike with the wind knocked out of me. He is staring at me, trying to figure out how he cut my leg off and where the hell it could be!"

Sometimes humor is the best medicine for stress. It's especially effective with children. I asked Theresa, the young woman who works with refugees, how the kids in a camp in Kosovo reacted to the stress of their situation, she said, "You won't believe this. The kids were hanging out. They were getting scolded by the adults in the camps for having fun during a war."

"They needed to connect with their peers for social support?"

"They needed normalcy. Feeling inhuman characterizes the refugee experience. It was important for them to return to activities that reminded them of stability, even though they've grown up with sustained instability. I mean this is the second war for most of them. Guess what the most popular theme for a youth club was?"

"Computers?"

"No. Comedy Club."

"They did stand-up comedy?"

"They did these little joke clubs. Is that fascinating?"

"It is!"

"What do you think the humor did for them? How did it help?"

"It helps them get their bearings. It gives them a sense of hope."

There is even some evidence that the positive emotional state and bodily changes (e.g. decreased muscle tension, reduction of stress hormones) that accompany laughter benefit physical health. In one Japanese study, cancer patients who watched a funny movie, and who thought it was funny, had a positive immune response (a higher concentration of cancer-battling natural killer cells).

The psychological attitude that laughter brings is, however, what is most important. If a child can laugh at a situation, it shows that she has some control over it. Laughter is affirming, non-defeatist and optimistic; it communicates that even in the face of adversity, one can find enjoyment.[9]

Living in the Present

One of the best life-skills we can impart to our children, one of the most effective immunizations against stress, is the ability to live in the present, informed by the past, but not its slave. In this chapter, I have tried to give parents greater insight into how to develop this approach to life in their kids.

Stress, disappointment, and loss bring opportunities to teach our kids how to move on, to pick themselves up when fate has knocked them over and keep going.

Our children need to believe that when they are hurt, frightened, or sad that they can do something that will lessen their emotional pain. They can draw inspiration from others who have walked a similar road, they can become more aware of their feelings and gain control over them, and they can learn to confront "unfinished business" and put bad feelings and false assumptions to rest.

We can help model for them important techniques for coping with stress. Like Theresa's Kosovo refugee kids or Jothy Rosenberg, they can learn to laugh when life seems difficult. Like George McGovern, they can learn to trust in the future. Like Steve Ross, they can put the past behind them and live life.

PART THREE

PART THREE

CHAPTER 7

———

Grace Under Pressure

To endure is the first thing a child ought to learn and that which he will
have the most need to know.

JEAN-JACQUES ROUSSEAU

Conversion Reaction

Just after I had returned from interviewing Theresa, I found
myself once again at the site of my post-traumatic stress
flashback: Boston's Brigham and Women's Hospital, where
Catalina was being seen for minor day surgery. As fate would
have it, day surgery at Brigham is located near the same
obstetrics unit where we had lost our first child. As we passed
familiar sites on the way to the day surgery waiting room,
Catalina and I exchanged glances of sad remembrance.

Catalina was wheeled into surgery just a few minutes
after noon. The surgeon had told us that the procedure would
take fifteen minutes and that the effects of the anesthesia
should take another hour or two to wear off. We figured we'd
have more than enough time to go together to pick up Diana

and Julia at school. But at 2:30, the waiting room nurse said that it would probably be another hour before Catalina was ready to be discharged. I told her that I had to go pick up the kids, and I asked her to tell Catalina that I would be back as soon as possible.

When I returned to the hospital at 4:15 with the kids, I was surprised when the nurse told me that Catalina was still in recovery and that it would be at least another forty-five minutes until she could be released. I wasn't concerned about Catalina's well-being. I know that she is more sensitive to medication than most people. I thought her system was just taking an atypically long time to recover.

The girls and I dined in the hospital cafeteria. But when we returned to the waiting room at 5:00, Catalina was still in recovery. I began to worry. I thanked my daughters for their patience and told them that they could watch television.

A nurse called me over. "Your wife is having trouble speaking," she said. I didn't like her tone. It was foreboding.

"A stroke in Broca's area?" I asked. The nurse looked perplexed. "I'm a neuropsychologist," I told her, which was essentially true. I had been a practicing clinical neuropsychologist until recently, although I had had little experience with adult stroke patients.

My words catalyzed the nurse. She ushered me into recovery and presented me and my credentials to the neurology resident who was on the case. "Not a stroke," he said, scribbling on Catalina's chart. "Conversion reaction. Probably for some secondary gain." Translated into English, this meant, roughly, "She's faking her symptoms because she doesn't want to go home."

I'll omit the details of the events that followed, the sloppy neurological exam by another sleep-deprived resident that confirmed the first diagnosis, my heated observation that when doctors don't really know what's going on they fall back on psychiatric explanations, and the perception by the resident that my anger confirmed his suspicion that my wife would rather be lying on a gurney in a hospital gown with IV tubes in her arms than home with me.

I spent the next hour or so shuttling back and forth between my anxious, speechless wife in the recovery room and my TV-happy kids in the waiting room. I told them that their mother wasn't talking, and that I suspected that it was an unusual reaction to the medication. I tried to project calm, and it appeared to work: they seemed fine.

At 7:30, the day surgery recovery room was closing. Everyone except Catalina had gone home.

"Are you going to admit her to the hospital?" I asked the neurologist.

"Not on a neurology ward," he replied (translation: "How can I? She doesn't have a neurological problem"). "I doubt that psychiatry would take her. We're going to send her to the recovery room for surgery inpatients."

I brought the children over to see their mom as she was wheeled out the door and down the hall. They held her hand. She smiled but couldn't say a word. It shook them to see their mother on a gurney, wearing a hospital gown, hooked up to an IV and unable to talk.

I made some phone calls and was fortunate to find Jed, a gracious friend who offered to come to the hospital, pick up the kids, and let them stay at his house. As we waited for him to arrive by the hospital entrance, the girls and I giggled, paying rhyming games and whispering made-up stories to each other about passersby: one was a spy; another, a pick-pocket; still another had gotten lost on his way to a pizza parlor.

I could feel their anxiety dissipate in the thirty minutes or so it took Jed to arrive. I was relieved to see that they weren't worried, that they were taking it in stride. It allowed me to concentrate on Catalina.

Around midnight, the neurologist decided that he had better image Catalina's brain after all and ordered an MRI. My original diagnosis was close to the mark. Catalina had had a cerebral hemorrhage in a brain area that affects speech. She was admitted to the hospital (on a neurology ward), where she remained for several days while the neurologists and neurosurgeons tried to figure out what had happened and what they should do about it. The tests they did ruled out lots of awful possibilities (a brain tumor, for example). But we are still not sure what caused the hemorrhage.

The neurology resident and I eventually mended our fences—the Brigham is, after all, a teaching hospital, and it is hard to learn unless you make mistakes. But by the time we had a diagnosis, I had spent a long stressful day (and night) at the hospital—and the stress was just beginning. I was faced with a logistical nightmare: a wife who couldn't speak, drive, work, or be left alone; who required daily trips to distant hospitals for rehabilitation and examinations once she got out of the hospital. Responsibility for Catalina's busy clinical psychology practice initially fell on me. I had to make sure that her patients were covered. Our two children had to be driven thirty minutes each way to school, as well as to sports and to music lessons. Speaking engagements took me to distant states. A book deadline loomed.

It's not surprising that I was worried. I worried about my wife (would she fully recover?) and my children (how could I keep them from falling apart?). I worried about myself (Could I handle this?).

Lessons from the Past

In the week that followed my dark night of the soul at Brigham and Women's Hospital, I often found myself thinking about Steve Ross in a concentration camp or what Prudence, Marion, or Sean McManus had to go through. I applied the lessons that I had learned from them about helping our kids cope with stress. I came to understand, firsthand, the importance of strong connections, humor, and looking at the big picture. I saw how important it is to give our children a sense that they have some control over how to deal with adversity, that they can manage a situation and their feelings about it, rather than feeling powerless. In addition, I learned (and tried to teach my children) something about accepting the things we can't change.

In this last chapter, I integrate the lessons I learned in my research and interviews with the remarkable people you met in Part Two.

I hadn't initially planned on ending this book like this. But then, neither had I planned on having my wife's routine day surgery turn into a protracted psychological stress test.

That, I suppose, is the first lesson I learned: You never know when stress immunization may come in handy.

A Strong Foundation

Human children (and this holds true as well for the young of many mammals) have a universal response to fear—they run to their mothers (or, sometimes, to their fathers). A clown-phobic child at the circus will cling to its mother with the same ferocity as a young baboon that smells a leopard. A child with a strong bond to his mother and father uses this secure attachment as a base from which to explore and a safe haven to return to when he gets scared.

My children had this secure base; I think most Millennial children do. Parents of this generation, in my experience, are pretty good about making sure that they have a strong emotional bond with their infants. We hold them (sometimes we don't ever want to let go), stay attuned to their needs (sometimes so much so that we don't let them go to sleep), and are ever vigilant about their safety.

Attachment does not stop with this essential early bonding experience. Growing children draw strength from their attachment to family, social groups, and their community. Research tells us that periods of stress, such as hard economic times, or in my case, a spouse's illness, often go hand in hand with family problems: divorce, neglect, abuse, or simply inattentive or irritable parenting. During these periods, mothers and fathers get stressed and depressed. They become less effective parents. They become less able to provide a secure, loving, structured, and supportive environment for their children. Social capital can help fill that void when parents become absorbed in their problems. There are periods in most of our lives when we are unable to extend ourselves, when we feel overwhelmed.

During Catalina's recovery I found myself digging deep into my reserve of social capital. Friends and neighbors picked up and dropped off my kids at school and sports practices. They cooked for us. They included Julia and Diana in outings. My children and I are much better off as a result, and we have grown closer to the people around us who were ready with a helping hand.

Hockey Parents and Poker Buddies

I didn't fully realize the extent of my family's social capital until Catalina's illness. This is because my social life is on the quiet side. I enjoy solitary pursuits and I am not much of a joiner. Thankfully, my wife has a more intricate web of social relations. When the news of her infirmity hit the streets, people came out of the woodwork with offers of help. We were flooded with lasagna. Flowers and visitors arrived at the hospital in droves. Within a few days, one of her colleagues had taken over the responsibility for her clinical caseload. Whenever I needed help with chauffeuring, there was always someone ready to pitch in. As Theresa, the refugee worker from Part Two, points out, people are hungry to help.

We need to figure out ways to become closer to each other, to share our lives. Since this is not my natural predisposition,

I've had to work to come out of myself. I have made a promise to myself to be more involved in the community, to socialize more, to drop in on the neighbors once in a while. In an effort to do this, I am coaching Julia's town softball team and Diana's school softball team this year. I applaud the efforts of one of our neighbors who, not long after the 9/11 attacks, threw a party and invited the neighborhood. Block parties and book clubs are effective ways of forming well-defined groups. This is the strength of life in Anna, Illinois, where the community gathers each morning for coffee and to gab. How much longer will that kind of life continue? Churches and synagogues used to provide this kind of community and cohesion.

Our strong predisposition to form groups, tribes, and clans runs deep into our history, extending into the animal packs from which we evolved.[1] I was unaware of how many of these groups I belonged to until Catalina was ill. I was surprised and moved when I realized what I was entitled to with membership in these groups.

My twelve-year-old daughter, Diana, plays for one of the finest girls' hockey programs in the country—Assabet Valley in Concord, Massachusetts. Even though she plays on the team with the lowest skill level for her age—Squirt Blue—the players and parents take vicarious pride in their association with the girls on the top team—Squirt Red—who are often in the hunt for the national championship, and the Olympians who formerly played on the Assabet home ice. Diana has a red and blue team jacket with her name on the sleeve and ASSABET written in large letters on the back.

Hockey is a time-intensive sport. The players are drawn

from several communities; many Squirt Blue parents have long commutes to games or practices. We parents spend hours shivering together in frigid ice rinks. Despite the fact that, for the most part, we have no connection outside hockey—we are not neighbors, our daughters do not attend the same schools—a bond has formed among us.

I realized this one day while driving my daughter to an evening practice. As I drove into the rink parking lot, I had a feeling of arriving home. It reminded me of the feelings I used to have when I was a regular churchgoer. The rink was a familiar place with familiar faces. It calmed me. I mentioned this to one of the parents as we sat in the dark stands, watching our daughters practice slap shots on the fresh ice. She told me that she felt the same way—the rink was a refuge for her, too.

The support we got from the team during my wife's recovery was phenomenal. Diana mentioned to a teammate in the locker room that Catalina was in the hospital. A mother secretly lacing her daughter's skates (self-sufficiency is expected at Assabet) overheard her, and the word was out. Hockey parents shuttled Diana back and forth to practice. They called to see if we needed anything. They sent cards to Catalina. The physical support that they gave us was helpful, but, even more important was the fact that I knew that they were there for us if we needed them.

It was the same with my poker buddies. I get together with them perhaps once every two months. We joke around and have a few beers. I rarely see most of the guys with whom I play outside this context. But as soon as they heard

Catalina was sick, they all called with offers of help. I was moved.

As we've seen, these kinds of groups are fundamental to human health and happiness, especially in times of trouble. I also learned firsthand that social capital reduces stress by providing direct material assistance (e.g., transportation), indirect connections to information and outside services ("My brother-in-law is a neurologist, if you need someone to . . ."), and monitoring ("Are you okay?").

We have a choice—disassociate or connect. We can be like the people that Theresa mentioned, who live anonymously in some inner-city Chicago neighborhoods, with few social connections and little social capital. Our urban and suburban lives are marked, in part, by isolation. In recent decades there has been an erosion of social capital in America, but the wise investor will not neglect this part of his portfolio.

Projecting Confidence

One of the few aspects of a stressful situation that parents have some control over is how they will react to it in front of their children. We have learned from the stories in Part Two that children are invariably grateful to their parents for being strong during tough times. That is part of a parent's job. Children, young ones especially, are extremely vulnerable. And vulnerability is at the root of fear. Fear and anxiety emanate from a feeling that we cannot manage a situation, that we don't have the resources to deal effectively with a given challenge. Test anxiety comes from the fear that you don't know the material. Fear of flying comes from the fear that you can't do anything about a crash. Fear of the dark emanates from the suspicion that there is something out there more powerful than you are.

When children's fears are allayed, their stress and trauma is reduced. We're able to lessen their fears when they believe we can protect them. This is our job, to project confidence even if we secretly have doubts. Summoning humor can be a potent way to reassure children that everything is, indeed, as it should be, and that, as parents, we're in control.

A way for us to project that things are going to be all right is to stick to routine. I followed this advice when my wife was in the hospital. My daughter Julia had been eagerly looking forward to attending a Harvard–Cornell women's basketball game. As it turned out, the game was a couple of days after Catalina had her hemorrhage. She was still in the hospital. Although Julia would have understood if we hadn't gone to the game, I decided to take her. This helped her feel that the world hadn't fallen apart. Just as Marion was impressed by her mother's ability to provide for the family at Christmas even though her father, the breadwinner, had died, I hoped that Julia would realize by my actions that although her mom was sick, all was not lost.

Father Involvement and the Family Dinner

In the research I conducted for my previous book, *Too Much of a Good Thing*, I found that families who eat dinner together on a regular basis are less likely to have a child who is depressed or using illegal drugs. A likely reason that family dinners promote a child's mental health is that the fathers in these families are involved in child rearing. Fathers are an important part of a child's fund of social capital.

I work hard to be an involved father. I am fortunate that I have the luxury of working mostly from home. Although my work calls for occasional travel, I am able to spend more time with my children than many fathers. Moreover, I have made a point of trying to be a full-service parent, capable of handling all facets of childcare. The best way for many fathers to accomplish this is on-the-job training.

Every year for the past four years, my daughters and I have taken a vacation together at the end of the summer. It started when my wife went to a yoga retreat in Montana. I decided that our family needed to balance its karmic quotient—for every yin, I reasoned, there must be an equal and opposite yang. So I rented a large motor home, and I took the girls on a safari of Midwestern water parks, wax museums, and other tacky tourist spots (racing go-karts and eating cotton candy is my idea of yang). We had a ball, and I learned a lot about being a full-time parent. The road trip tradition has continued, and the girls and I now know how to function as a trio.

When my wife became incapacitated, I had little difficulty handling the day-to-day chores of parenting. My children's routines were kept intact. There was little needed adaptation. Moreover, I didn't use up all my energy trying to get up to speed on the daddy track.

The equilibrium my children felt during Catalina's illness

came, in part, from the competence I had developed during our annual motor home vacations. They intuitively knew that I could care for them by myself. This feeling, of course, was not unconditional. The loss of their mother would have left a gaping hole in their world that I could not hope to fill.

I strongly encourage fathers to become involved in the details of parenting. We need to know our children's shoe sizes, what to do if they get sick, the whens and wheres of their weekly schedules, and how to make their favorite foods (or at least where to get adequate take-out). For wives reading this and asking themselves, "How can I get my husband more involved?" my answer is, "Get out of the way and let your husband have some on-the-job training." If you can afford it, go to Bermuda by yourself for a week. If not, just get out of the house and leave him with the kids once in a while (more than one day is best). Everyone in the family will benefit.

Giving Children a Sense of Control

In addition to projecting that you have stressful situations under control, that you have the competence to meet the challenges at hand, a parent also needs to help the child feel competent—and it helps if this feeling isn't an illusion. I saw this come to light after Catalina came home from the hospital. I did my best to encourage my kids to participate in her recovery. Julia decided that she was going to teach Catalina how to talk again.

"What grade level should I start her at, Daddy?" she asked me.

"Well," I said, "we're going to have to test her."

"You mean to see what words she knows?"

"Exactly."

Julia looked through her books. "Do you think I should use Dr. Seuss or Nancy Drew?"

Julia then set up a little school with blackboard, desk, and chair in our basement. She worked on sentence completion with Catalina and put together homework assignments for her.

Diana made sure that Catalina was following doctor's orders. "Mom, you know the doctor says you need to sit down when you take a shower," she would remind Catalina. "You might fall down." Catalina tried to convince Diana she could shower by herself. But Diana held firm. "I'll bring a chair into the shower for you. And don't worry, I'll sit in the bathroom with you to make you sure you're okay."

I did have my suspicion that Diana took a secret delight in this reversal of roles. But there wasn't a trace of this in Diana's solicitousness—just protectiveness and love. And the sense that she was part of the solution.

It's important that we encourage our children and make them see that they aren't helpless, that there will almost always be something they can do by themselves and for themselves to deal with stress. We want our kids to know that even if they have no control over what's causing stress, they can at least do something about how they respond to it.

We should teach our kids a systematic coping style. When faced with a stressful situation, we need to give our kids practice in defining the problem as specifically as possible. Many kids wilt under pressure because they see a situation or task as overwhelming. When a child has a large school project looming, for example, he'll say, "I can't do this" or "I'll never get this done on time." We need to help children break down problems into manageable parts. We should teach them to look at their options. Perhaps they don't have the materials they need. Perhaps they're running out of time. Perhaps they're unclear on what they have to do.

Once a problem is defined in a realistic way it becomes less overwhelming. If it's broken down into pieces, it's easier to deal with. When children see that the problem is not as overwhelming as they thought, they usually gain confidence and begin to feel like the puppeteer rather than the puppet.

Courage

One strategy I have used to help my children develop a sense of competence, that they have capacities they didn't know they had, is to give them "bravery tests." One fall day I took them to the Metropolitan Museum in New York City. We were in the entrance hall, sitting on a bench, waiting for their grandmother to finish touring the gift shop. The museum was crowded; the stimulation threatened to overwhelm them. They were also antsy and starting to drive me crazy. So I started issuing challenges. Spying a large, scowling, tattooed man with a bushy beard sitting by himself (a novel entity for two private-school girls living in a bucolic suburban neighborhood), I said, "I'll give you a dollar if you go ask that man if you can have his hat."

Their eyes widened, riveted on his fearsome visage. Their little bodies stiffened. Suddenly they were focused and still.

"No way," they said in tandem.

"Okay," I said. "Just go ask him what time it is."

They thought about that one for a second. "I don't think so," Diana finally replied. Julia nodded emphatically.

Eventually, they mustered up enough courage to meet my challenge of walking to a large pillar ten steps in the direction of this child-devouring goblin. They returned breathing hard with a wild look in their eyes. So I pushed a little harder (I had dropped the financial reward; I told them I was only willing to pay for the scowling man's Harley Davidson hat).

"Now see if you can walk over and touch the wall" (another ten steps past the pillar). This, too, was accomplished with some trepidation. Eventually their fear began to dissipate and they accepted new challenges. Julia passed the test of walking over to the information booth and asking for a map. Diana snaked her way through the crowd over to the entrance of the Egyptian wing and came back with the information written on a distant sign.

I have continued to employ similar bravery tests in other situations. Children often learn that they are more capable than they had imagined. They love to see progress and feel that they have overcome their fears (just as they are overjoyed to see they have grown when we measure their height with pencil marks on a wall). I time my children as they run through obstacle courses which I have constructed for them. They enjoy seeing their times go down.

Find out a child's capacity and then stretch it. It is the same principle employed by any good teacher or psychotherapist. People learn best when the challenge presented is in their "zone of proximal development," a kind of inside way of saying, "only what they are ready for, not too easy and not too hard." Children can often be very good informants about where they are when it comes to mastering fears.

I have employed this with children who have difficulty going to sleep alone. One child was very organized about what she needed. She told me that it would be "a three-step process." The first week she wanted someone in bed with her while she fell asleep. The next week, the person would sit in a chair in her room while she fell asleep. The third week they would stand by the door as she dozed off. Then she felt she could face going to sleep alone.

This is the same procedure that behavior therapists use to cure phobias, such as fear of snakes. The procedure is called "systematic desensitization." In this process, the therapist creates a fear hierarchy and helps the patient learn to relax in the presence of increasingly frightening stressors. To treat a fear of snakes, for example, the therapist may first have the patient relax while looking at a small picture of a nonpoisonous snake in a magazine. With gradual treatment, the patient will soon be able to relax while looking at a larger picture of a poisonous snake. Eventually some patients will be able to hold and handle snakes without fear.

Humor

Laughter can dispel a feeling of helplessness. Being able to view a stressful situation with humor ("At least I can laugh about it") denotes some measure of control over it. Humor has helped both me and my children keep a positive attitude during my wife's recovery.

At first, Catalina could only manage the words *yes* and *no*. Her particular brain lesion made it impossible for her to "find words." She could, however, immediately repeat what was said to her. So I started giving her sentences to repeat. I tried simple sentences in both English and Spanish: "I am hungry"; *"Tengo hambre."* She had no trouble with these. Then, when my children first visited her in the hospital, I asked her to repeat sentences such as, "Julia and Diana deserve more allowance," and "Julia and Diana should get to watch more TV."

Catalina repeated these flawlessly and was amused to hear herself say sentences she had never said before. It felt good to laugh, and it felt even better to hear the laughter of my wife and children.

Catalina's language began to improve slowly, and by the time she came home, she could sometimes manage simple sentences on her own. More commonly, she got two or three words of a sentence out and then got stuck. The girls and I would then try to guess what she wanted to say. Our lives became an endless game of charades. One of the first phrases Catalina mastered was "Do me a favor and . . ." at which point she would run out of words and we would start guessing—"Get you something to eat?" "Get your medicine?"—until one of us would get it right (Diana became the household charades master).

On one occasion, Catalina said, "Do me a favor and . . ."

"Get lost?" Julia said with perfect comedic timing. We all cracked up. From that point on, "Get lost" became our catchphrase.

For our family, laughter was often the best medicine. It

made our collective burden lighter and brought us closer. Like the refugee children's creation of a comedy club in Kosovo, our family had a bad situation to deal with and we chose to laugh in its face.

Caveats

This seems like a good time to add a caveat. Thus far, I have given suggestions for what to do rather than what to avoid. Parents should also keep in mind that research has shown that some coping techniques to stress or trauma tend to be counterproductive. "Venting" or unregulated emotional discharge, such as yelling or screaming, has been consistently found to be associated with psychological problems and a lack of competence in dealing with stress. Part of the reason for this is that children who can "control themselves" are less likely to be overwhelmed by the negative emotions that may accompany stress.[2] We need to teach our children the skills to deal with strong feelings. We shouldn't sit on our feelings, but we should try to express our negative emotions in positive ways. Father McManus is a sterling example of this. He turned his anger and grief into political activism and compassionate theology.

An added benefit, of course, is that kids who know how to regulate their anger tend to have more friends and be better liked by adults than their more volatile peers.

We also need to guard against our children becoming too self-critical—blaming themselves for stress or trauma that has nothing to do with them. As with "venting," it is the *unregulated* aspect of self-criticism that is psychologically damaging.[3] It is fine for a child to be introspective, to examine her actions, to use past failures as motivation to do better. What isn't healthy is for self-criticism to become total or permanent.

Parents should be alert for attitudes or statements that indicate that a child is feeling that he's totally bad (or incompetent, stupid, unattractive, etc.) and will *always* be that way. These kinds of statements or attitudes should be challenged. The parent should try to get the child to see that he has some measure of control, that he isn't powerless, and, most importantly, that the condition is changeable or temporary.

Productive Passivity

There are, of course situations that we can't change. It is important for a parent to help a child recognize these, because at these times the best coping strategy will often be acceptance or resignation. This was graphically illustrated for me by a story George McGovern told me about one of his war experiences as a bomber pilot.

"During combat I knew that there was nothing I could do to avoid anti-aircraft fire," McGovern said. "It was a matter of fate. You just had to fly straight. Once you got to the target area, you had to fly straight and level, and the flak, well, you wouldn't think you could get through. It would be jet-black ahead of you from the anti-aircraft shells, except for the bright red flashes of fire at the moment of the impact. I think one of the impacts it had on me is that from that point on in my life I figured [that] if I was going to do something, I'd better get started today because you don't know whether tomorrow is going to come."

Children (or adults, for that matter) who erroneously believe that they can control uncontrollable events are often worse off than those who resign themselves to their fate. People who fear flying, for example, may suffer more when they remain vigilant while airborne—as if they were actually influencing what is happening to the plane—than if they adopt a fatalistic attitude.

In her classic study of British children affected by the Blitz, *War and Children*, Anna Freud relates a story of a mother and a son waiting out a particularly bad air raid in a London underground station.[4] The mother listened keenly for every explosion, seemingly trying to will the bombs away. After a few minutes her young son began reading the book he had brought along, much to the mother's consternation. Finally she could stand it any longer and told him "Put down your book and attend to the air raid!" Dr. Freud uses this example to let parents know that in some situations it is best for us to let children accept their situation and even actively work to ignore it.

More recent wartime research bears out Dr. Freud's conclusions. Israeli children confined in a sealed room (as protection against biological weapon attacks during air raids in the Gulf War) who distracted themselves or engaged in wishful thinking showed fewer signs of stress after the war was over than their peers who focused on what was going on around them.[5]

An interesting sidebar to the Gulf War study is that

younger children (fifth graders) tended to have more difficulty coping with the stress of the attack than older children
(seventh and tenth graders). As I discussed in Chapter Two,
the younger kids had the disadvantage of having what film-
maker Woody Allen likes to call a "faulty denial mechanism." They had a harder time distorting reality; it was more
difficult for them to slip into denial about the danger they
were in.

Downward Social Comparison

I knew that despite the severity of my wife's illness, the challenge of coping with it (for me anyway) was nothing in comparison to the adversity I had heard about from some of the
people I interviewed: Nazi concentration camps, disease pan-
demics, and political oppression. When I thought of the hor-
rors endured by my interviewees, I felt better. I am not quite
sure why comparing ourselves to those less fortunate than
ourselves helps in times of stress, but it can be effective in some
instances, perhaps because it gives us a sense of perspective.

The mother of all downward social comparison stories is
the Biblical story of Job. Satan bets God that if Job was
stripped of his wealth, family, and health, Job would curse
God. God accepts the challenge. He allows Satan to rob Job
of his wealth and kill Job's children. But Job does not lose
faith. He resigns himself, saying that "the Lord gives and the
Lord takes away." Satan then covers Job from head to foot
with running sores and turns Job's friends against him. Job

curses the day he was born. "Why is life given to men who find it so bitter?" he asks. Yet he never curses God, and his righteousness is rewarded. God doubles the amount of all Job's former possessions. Job has ten more children and lives another one hundred forty years.

At one level, the story is meant as an inspiration to those who are suffering, telling them that no matter how hard their lives become, they can cope as long as their faith remains strong. Job helps us get perspective on our suffering: it can't be as bad as what he had to endure (or what Steve Ross had to endure, for that matter). Job is the quintessential instance of the coping method psychologists call downward social comparison.[6]

––––––––––

As we've seen, Millennial children lack this perspective. They have extremely high expectations for comfort, health, and happiness. It's important that we give them some perspective on where they stand. I try to help my children—in a non–guilt inducing, non-punitive way—understand how fortunate they are.

I have drawn charts for my kids to show them how wealthy we are vis-à-vis the rest of the world. They were stunned, sheltered as they are, to see how comparatively rich we are. Why wouldn't they be? Many of their classmates live in nicer homes than we do, take more expensive vacations, and drive fancier cars. It's up to us to tell our children how privileged their lives are. Recognizing this privilege can help them cope with tough times. They will tend to be less self-pitying. They will be able to put their difficulties in perspective.

Outward Bound (or similar programs) can also have this salutary effect. Kids are pushed to their physical limits. They go hungry. They have to live without the comforts of home—cars, televisions, computers. For many kids, a rigorous, survival-focused outdoor program can change their lives. It helps them develop a sense of their own endurance.

Perhaps a kinder, gentler way to instill the same message is through a different kind of family vacation. A family I know recently took their thirteen- and nine-year-old kids on a work vacation to Mexico. They lived in a small house in a poor neighborhood on the outskirts of Oaxaca; they worked long hours, pouring concrete to help build a clinic. The kids came back enriched and strengthened. They realized how privileged they were. They also realized there were other, simpler ways to live.

Look at the Big Picture

Giving our children the feeling that their life has purpose and meaning may be the hardest recommendation to carry out, but, in the end, it may be the most important. If we can answer our children's existential questions we will give them an internal compass, which will be a potent tool for coping with stress, not to mention pointing them toward the possibility of true happiness.

Many of us who are religious have that internal compass. When our children ask us about the purpose of life, we have answers, a big picture that's already in place. If we're Christians, for example, we can tell our kids how, by aligning themselves with Christ's teachings, they can lead a good life and go to heaven when they die. But how can those of us who are part of the growing secular trend—lukewarm believers, agnostics, or atheists—instill a deep purpose in our children that will guide them when they're faced with the suffering and disillusionment that is an inevitable part of life?

The godfather of existential psychology, Viktor Frankl, author of *Man's Search for Meaning*, his classic book on his experiences in a Nazi concentration camp, identifies two primary sources of meaning (other than suffering): doing or creating something, most often to benefit another, and the experience of love or other transcendent feelings.[7]

Frankl's book addresses adult concerns, but his insights can help us answer our children's existential questions. By living Frankl's first point, we transmit to our children through word and deed that doing things for others is important and a way to give life meaning and experience fulfillment. We can help our children develop the impulse to give by requiring them to set aside a portion of their allowances. If your child's allowance is $5 a week, make sure a set percentage (somewhere between 5 and 20 percent) goes into a charitable account. You can explore together which charity should be the beneficiary of your child's largesse. In a similar vein, parents can encourage children to care for people who are ill by sending cards, visiting them, or drawing pictures as gifts.

Frankl's second point is crucial. Love is the center of our lives. Without it we are truly lost. The first love a child will experience comes from his parents. These feelings should be transmitted from parent to child through close physical contact, declarations of love, and a deep acceptance of the child.

Sometimes, especially as children get older, the hectic pace of life, quotidian irritations, and overscheduling detract from the enjoyment family members take in each other. Our interactions too often center on unfinished homework, undone chores, and debates over rules and restrictions. Love can get lost in the shuffle. It's vitally important to schedule time with each child, one on one, doing things that you *both* enjoy. Many parents and children find that these special times allow them to rekindle their mutual feeling of love and strengthen the connection between them.

Pets are a good way to expose our children's latent capacity to love and nurture. When I see my daughters stroking their cats and cooing to them in the language we reserve for pets and babies, I see them in rehearsal for the time when they will be steeped in the transcendent love for their children.

The love we give our children can stay with them and provide strength and purpose. Our own children will carry it with them when they face tough times. It will give them the foundation to create the deep sense of connectedness to each other and to life that is the best defense against darkness and despair. It will center them when they are floundering. In itself it can be the internal compass that will guide them toward meaning and purpose.

Conclusion

There is a happy ending to the story of my wife's illness. Catalina has made a full recovery. She regained her speech relatively quickly. She is able to drive again. Her coordination is back. She has gone back to work. The kids are fine, and so am I.

The events of 9/11 and Catalina's illness are bookends for me, marking the necessity of teaching my own children resilience and strength in the face of adversity. We want our children to be able to cope with grief and fear. We want them to be able to make the best out of bad situations. We want our children to feel whole, useful, and engaged—fully participatory in the life of the world.

We need to look at how we, as parents, can give our kids the kind of inner strength that they'll need to face the challenges ahead. I hope this book has been useful in this respect. Resilient children derive their strength from strong family ties and character-building experiences. This doesn't mean boot-camp discipline and spanking. It doesn't mean having impossible expectations for them. But it does mean remaining calm, optimistic, and resolute in the face of adversity, modeling grace under pressure, not succumbing to petty irritations, showing them love, connecting them to the wider world, taking the time to understand what they're thinking and feeling, giving them a sense of how fortunate they are, and helping them find meaning and purpose in life.

CODA

DAN: What was it like for you when your mom was in the hospital?

JULIA: Don't you want to close the door?

DAN: Good idea. Okay. Tell me what it was like for you the day that we were there at the Brigham. Were you worried about Mom?

JULIA: Well, at first I wasn't so worried because I didn't know anything was wrong.

DAN: You got scared later?

JULIA: Yeah, later when I started to get what was going on.

DAN: What helped you not to be scared?

JULIA: Well, being with you was good.

DAN: That helped to make you feel better?

JULIA: Yes.

DAN: What about me being there made you feel better?

JULIA: Having fun was the best part.

DAN: What fun?

JULIA: The rhyming game we played. Remember?

DAN: You mean while we were waiting for Jed to pick you up?

JULIA: Remember? You said, "See that man all dressed in green?" And I said, "He's doing a dog pose by the washing machine."

DAN: [laughs]

JULIA: And the basketball game? That was a lot of fun. That helped take my mind off things.

DAN: So it didn't seem so bad. How about September 11? Tell me about that day.

JULIA: Now that was [nervous laugh], that was bad. You not being there was the worst.

DAN: What did Mom do to make it better?

JULIA: She talked to me and calmed me down.

DAN: What else helped you not to be so scared?

JULIA: When we were all together again after you came home. And, like, talking and comforting myself.

DAN: How did you comfort yourself?

JULIA: By going into the closet.

DAN: What did you do in there?

JULIA: I looked up words in the dictionary that I didn't know.

DAN: You took the light and the dictionary in there?

JULIA: Yeah. I had a little book for writing words in. And a pencil. It's still in there.

DAN: To write down words you didn't know.

JULIA: To keep myself from thinking about being scared.

DAN: So you created a little space for yourself in the closet?

JULIA: It was a very good fit.

DAN: How about going to sleep at night? What's helped you with that?

JULIA: My "thinks" help a lot. But having someone in the room is also pretty good.

DAN: Tell me about your thinks.

JULIA: Well, I just think of a good subject. Like a soccer game playing in my head. Sometimes I do things that are impossible. I put my arms out and fly around.

DAN: Where do you go?

JULIA: When?

DAN: When you fly.

JULIA: Over the town.

DAN: You fly over Sudbury?

JULIA: Yes!

DAN: That sounds like good fun.

JULIA: And having Beary [her teddy bear] helps.

DAN: How about Fluffy?

JULIA: She's a tremendous help.

DAN: What advice would you would give to kids who get scared? Or who have to go through tough times? Like having a parent who's sick or a divorce. What would you tell them?

JULIA: Try to have fun. But it matters what happened.

DAN: What if it was like September 11?

JULIA: I'd tell them to try to stay together with their family. And, if they had trouble, to try to talk things over with their parents.

DAN: What if you were the parent? If you had two little kids? What would you do?

JULIA: Try to comfort them if they were scared. And try to have a lot of fun. Like maybe take them out for ice cream.

ENDNOTES

CHAPTER 1
The End of Innocence

1. See for example, Stichick, T. (2001), "The psychosocial impact of armed conflict on children: Rethinking traditional paradigms in research and intervention," *Child and Adolescent Psychiatric Clinics of North America*, 10, 797–814.

2. A good recent summary of Norman Garmezy's resilience research can be found in Garmezy, N., "Reflections and commentary on risk, resilience and development," in R. J. Haggerty, L. R. Sherrod, N. Garmezy, and M. Rutter, eds., *Stress, Risk, and Resilience in Children and Adolescents: Processes, Mechanisms, and Interventions* (Cambridge, U.K.: Cambridge University Press), 1996, pp. 1–18.

3. Shorter, E. (1996), "Primary Care," in R. Porter (ed.) *The Cambridge Illustrated History of Medicine*, (Cambridge U.K.: Cambridge University Press), pp. 118–153. See especially page 151.

4. Quoted in a review of *The 70's: The Decade that Brought You Modern Life (For Better or Worse).* Oshinsky, D. M. "How We Got Here," *New York Times Book Review,* March 12, 2002, p. 13.

5. See Sax, J. L.; Astin, A. W.; Korn, W. S.; and Mahoney, K. M. *The American Freshmen: National Norms for Fall, 1998,* Los Angeles: Higher Education Research Institute University of California at Los Angeles, 1998.

6. Personal communication, David Rockefeller Jr., November 2001.

7. President Kennedy said this in a speech on May 18, 1963.

8. Statistics are taken from page 123 of Putnam, R. D., *Bowling Alone: The Collapse and Revival of American Community*, New York: Simon and Schuster, 2000.

9. Barzun, J., *From Dawn to Decadence: 500 Years of Western Cultural Life, 1500 to the Present,* New York: HarperCollins, 2000. See page 10.

10. *ibid.* page 28.

11. See Putnam, R. D., *Bowling Alone: The Collapse and Revival of American Community*, New York: Simon and Schuster, 2000.

12. Hofferth, S. L. (1999), "Changes in Children's time 1981–1997," *Center Survey*, 9, no. 1. Hofferth reports on her research conducted at the University of Michigan over the course of sixteen years beginning in 1981. Children's free time has declined 16 percent over this period (from 63 hours per week to 51 hours per week) and time not spent in school or doing regular activities such as eating and sleeping is more structured. Churchgoing declined 40 percent during this period, averaging 2.3 hours per week in 1981 and 1.2 hours in 1997. Most remarkable was that household conversation declined from 1 hour 12 minutes per week to 36 minutes per week. Sports participation doubled, going from 2 hours 20 minutes to 5 hours 17 minutes per week for the average child.

13. See pages 217–221 in Kindlon, D., *Too Much of a Good Thing: Raising Children of Character in an Indulgent Age*, New York: Talk Miramax Books, 2001.

CHAPTER 2
Children, Stress, and Coping

1. I drew on two articles that studied the psychological effects of Hurricane Andrew: Shaw, J. A.; Applegate, B.; Tanner, S.; Perez, D.; Rothe, E.; et al. (1995), "Psychological Effects of Hurricane Andrew on an Elementary School Population," *Journal of the American Academy of Child and Adolescent Psychiatry*, 34, 1185–1192; and Garrison, C. Z., et al. (1995), "Posttraumatic Stress Disorder in Adolescents after Hurricane Andrew," *Journal of the American Academy of Child and Adolescent Psychiatry*, 34, 1193–1201. Other research that has examined psychological symptoms in children a year after a natural disaster generally finds rates of trauma ranging between 0 percent and 37 percent. One notable exception is the finding of rates of depression and posttraumatic stress disorder well over 75 percent $1\frac{1}{2}$ years after the horrendous Spitak earthquake that killed as many as 100,000 people in December, 1988. (See report in Goenjian, A. K. et al. [1995], "Psychiatric Comorbidity in Children after the 1988 Earthquake in Armenia," *Journal of the American Academy of Child and Adolescent Psychiatry*, 34, 1174–1184.)

2. Terr, Lenore C., M.D.; Bloch, Daniel A., Ph.D.; Michel, Beat A., M.D.; Shi, Hong, M. S.; Reinhardt, John A., Ph.D.; Metayer, Suzanne (1999), "Children's Symptoms in the Wake of Challenger; A Field Study of Distant-Traumatic Effects and an Outline of Related Conditions," *The American Journal of Psychiatry*, 156, 1536–1544.

3. See, for example Garbarino, J.; and Sherman, D. (1980), High-risk neighborhoods and high-risk families: The human ecology of family maltreatment, *Child Development*, 51, 188–198. and Stichick, T. (2001), "The psychosocial impact of armed conflict on children: Rethinking traditional paradigms in research and intervention," *Child and Adolescent Psychiatric Clinics of North America*, 10, 797–814.

4. Two excellent reviews of progress in research on stress and coping in children are Compas, Bruce E.; Connor-Smith, Jennifer K.; Saltzman, Heidi; Thomsen, Alexandra Harding; and Wadsworth, Martha E. (2001), "Coping With Stress During Childhood and Adolescence: Problems, Progress, and Potential in Theory and Research," *Psychological Bulletin 227*(1): 87–127; and Haggerty, R. J.; Sherrod, L. R.; Garmezy, N.; and Rutter, M.; eds., *Stress, Risk, and Resilience in Children and Adolescents: Processes, Mechanisms, and Interventions* (pps. i–xxi). Cambridge, U.K.: Cambridge University Press. For a more general review see: Somerfield, M. R. and McCrae, R. R. (2000) "Stress and Coping Research Methodological Challenges, Theoretical Advances, and Clinical Applications," *American Psychologist*, 55, 620–625.

5. Lifetime prevalence of PTSD is stated to be between 1 and 14 percent in DSM-IV: American Psychiatric Association, *Diagnostic and Statistical Manual of Mental Disorders*, Fourth Edition, Washington, D.C.: American Psychiatric Association. In the National Comorbidity Survey, a representative sample of 5,877 Americans aged 15–54, the lifetime prevalence of PTSD was found to be 7.8 percent: Kessler, R. C.; Sonnega, A.; Bromet, E.; Hughes, M.; and Nelson, C. B. (1995), "Posttraumatic Stress Disorder in the National Comorbidity Survey," *Archives of General Psychiatry*, 52, 1048–1060. The lifetime prevalence of PTSD in a sample of 384 white, working-class eighteen-year-olds was 6.3 percent: Giaconia, R. M., et al. (1995), "Traumas and Posttraumatic Stress Disorder in a Community Population of Older Adolescents," *Journal of the American Academy of Child and Adolescent Psychiatry*, 34, 1369–1380. For prevalence of PTSD in teens and data on adult exposure to stress see page 5 of van der Kolk, B. A. "Preface," in van der Kolk, B. A.; McFarlane, A. C.; and Weisaeth, L., eds., *Traumatic Stress: The Effects of Overwhelming Experience on Mind, Body, and Society*, New York: The Guilford Press, 1996.

6. Primary sources used for this section on the biology of stress are Chrousos, George P., and Gold, Philip W. (1992), "The Concepts of Stress and Stress System Disorders: Overview of Physical and Behavioral Homeostasis," *JAMA*, 267, 1244–1252; and Henry, J. P. (1992), "Biological basis of the stress response," *Integrative Physiological and Behavioral Science*, 27, 66–83. An excellent, easy-to-read account of the biology of the stress response and the adverse consequences of chronic stress can be found in Sapolsky, R. M., *Why Zebras Don't Get Ulcers: An Updated Guide to Stress, Stress-Related Diseases, and Coping*, New York: W. H. Freeman, 1994.

7. Cohen, Sheldon; Tyrell, David A. J.; and Smith, Andrew P. (1991), "Psychological Stress and Susceptibility to the Common Cold," *The New England Journal of Medicine 325* (9): 606–612. Results show a dose-response increase in respiratory infection and clinical colds according to the degree of psychological stress.

8. See McEwen, B. B. (1998), "Protective and Damaging Effects of Stress Mediators: Allostasis and Allostatic Load," *Seminars in Medicine of the Beth*

Israel Deaconess Medical Center: Protective and Damaging Effects of Stress Mediators, 338, 171–179, and Schulkin, Jay; McEwen, Bruce; Gold, Philip (1994), "Allostasis, Amygdala, and Anticipatory Angst," *Neuroscience and Biobehavioral Reviews, 18* (3): 385–396.

9. Bremner, Douglas J.; Randall, Penny; Scott, Tammy M.; Broen, Richard A.; Seibyl, John P.; Southwick, Steven M.; Delaney, Richard C.; McCarthy, Gregory; Charney, Dennis S.; and Innish, Robert B. (1995), "MRI-Based Measurement of Hippocampal Volume in Patients with Combat-Related Posttraumatic Stress Disorder," *American Journal of Psychiatry,* 152(7): 973–981.

10. Taylor, S. E. et al. (2000), "Biobehavioral responses to stress in females tend-and-befriend not fight-or-fight," *Psychological Review*, 107, 411–429.

11. Primary sources for for this section are Terr, L. *Too Scared to Cry*, New York: Basic Books, 1990; and B. A. van der Kolk, A. C. McFarlane, and L. Weisaeth, eds., *Traumatic Stress: The Effects of Overwhelming Experience on Mind, Body, and Society*, New York: The Guilford Press, 1996.

12. Diagnostic criteria for PTSD taken from American Psychiatric Association: *Diagnostic and Statistical Manual of Mental Disorders*, Fourth Edition, Washington. D.C.: American Psychiatric Association.

13. See Garrison, W. T., and McQuiston, S., *Chronic Illness During Childhood and Adolescence: Psychological Aspects*, New York: Sage Publications, 1989.

14. Quote is from page 13 of Holliday, Laurel, *Children of "The Troubles": Our Lives in the Crossfire of Northern Ireland*, New York, Pocket Books, 1997.

15. More on McGovern's reactions to his daughter's death can be found in the compelling book: McGovern, George, *Terry: My Daughter's Life and Death Struggle with Alcoholism*, New York: Penguin, 1997.

16. A primary source for the section on temperament is Kagan, J., "Biology and the Child," in W. Damon and N. Eisenberg, eds., *Handbook of Child Psychology, fifth edition, Volume 3: Social, Emotional, and Personality Development.* (177–236), New York: John Wiley and Sons, 1998.

17. Sources used in writing the section on age-related changes in coping include Garrison, W. T., and McQuiston, S., *Chronic Illness During Childhood and Adolescence: Psychological Aspects*, New York: Sage Publications, 1989; Rutter, M. "Stress Research: Accomplishments and Tasks Ahead," in Haggerty, R. J.; Sherrod, L. R.; Garmezy, N.; and Rutter, M., eds., *Stress, Risk, and Resilience in Children and Adolescents: Processes, Mechanisms, and Interventions*, Cambridge, U.K.: Cambridge University Press, 1996, pp. 354–386; Haggerty, R. J. and Sherrod, L. R., "Preface," in Haggerty, R. J., Sherrod, L. R.; Garmezy, N., and Rutter, M. eds., *Stress, Risk, and Resilience in Children and Adolescents: Processes, Mechanisms, and Interventions*, Cambridge, U.K.: Cambridge University Press, 1996, pp. i–xxi.

18. See Burke, J. D.; Borus, J. F.; and Burns, B. J. (1982), "Changes in Chil-

dren's Behavior After a Natural Disaster," *American Journal of Psychiatry,* 139, 725–730. and Taylor, S. E. and Brown, J. D. (1988), "Illusion and well-being: A social psychological perspective on mental health," *Psychological Bulletin,* 103, 193–210.

19. Stewart, K., "Dream Theory in Malaya," in (C. Tart ed.) *Altered States of Consciousness,* New York: Doubleday Anchor, 1969, pp. 161–170.

20. Inauguration speech as published in Samuel Rosenman, ed., *The Public Papers of Franklin D. Roosevelt. Volume Two: The Year of Crisis, 1933,* New York: Random House, 1938, pp. 11–16.

21. Henry, J. P. (1992), Biological basis of the stress response, *Integrative Physiological and Behavioral Science,* 27, 66–83.

22. The classic book on learned helplessness is: Seligman, M. E. P., *Helplessness: On Development, Depression, and Death,* New York: HarperCollins, 1975/1992.

CHAPTER 3
The Ties That Bind

1. This research is discussed in: Sapolsky, R. M., *Why Zebras Don't Get Ulcers: An Updated Guide to Stress, Stress-Related Diseases, and Coping,* New York: W. H. Freeman, 1994.

2. Arnetz, B. B.; Edgren B.; Levi L. and Otto U. (1985) "Behavioural and Endocrine Reactions in Boys Scoring High on Sennton Neurotic Scale Viewing an Exciting and Partly Violent Movie and the Importance of Social Support," *Social Science & Medicine,* 20, 731–736.

3. The classic paper on this relation is House, J. S.; Landis, K. R.; and Umberson, D. (1988), "Social relationships and health," *Science,* 241, 540–545. See also a recent review: Uchino, B.; Cacioppo, J. T.; and Kiecolt-Glaser, J. K. (1996), "The Relationship Between Social Support and Physiological Processes: A Review with Emphasis on Underlying Mechanisms and Implications for Health," *Psychological Bulletin,* 119, 488–531.

4. Levy, S. M. et al. (1990), "Perceived Social Support and Tumor Estrogen/ Progesterone Receptor Status as Predictors of Natural Killer Cell Activity in Breast Cancer Patients," *Psychosomatic Medicine* 52, 73–85.

5. See House, J. S. (2001), "Social isolation kills, but how and why?" *Psychosomatic Medicine,* 63, 273–274: "[O]ur understanding of how and why social isolation is risky for health—or conversely—how and why social isolation is risky for health, still remains quite limited"; and House, J. S.; Landis, K. R.; and Umberson, D. (1988), "Social Relationships and Health," *Science* 241, 540–545.

6. For primary source on attachment see Thompson, R. A., "Early Sociopersonality Development," in W. Damon and N. Eisenberg, eds., *Handbook of Child Psychology, Fifth Edition, Volume 3: Social, Emotional, and Personality Development,* New York: John Wiley and Sons, 1998, pp. 25–104; Thompson,

R. A. (2000), "The legacy of early attachments," *Child Development,* 71, 145–152; Masten, A. S. and Coatsworth, J. D. (1998), "The Development of Competence in Favorable and Unfavorable Environments: Lessons from Research on Successful Children," *American Psychologist,* 53, 205–220; and Ainsworth, M. D. S. and Bowlby, J. (1991), "An Ethological Approach to Personality Development," *American Psychologist, 46,* 333–341.

7. Bachu, A. and O'Connell, M., *Fertility of American Women.* (Tech. Rep.), Washington, D.C., U.S. Census Bureau, 2000.

8. Brooks-Gunn, J.; Wen-Jai, H.; and Waldfogel, J. (2002), "Maternal Employment and Child Cognitive Outcome in the First Three Years of Life: The NICHD Study of Early Child Care," *Child Development* 73, 1052–1072.

9. Sagi, A.; Koren-Karie, N.; Gini, M.; Ziv, Y., and Joels, T. (2002), "Shedding Further Light on the Effects of Various Types and Quality of Early Child Care on Infant-Mother Attachment Relationship: The Haifa Study of Early Child Care," *Child Development,* July 2002.

10. See for example: Ainsworth, M. D. S. and Bowlby, J. (1991), "An ethological approach to personality development," *American Psychologist,* 46, 333–341.

11. Chisholm, K. (1998), "A Three-Year Follow-up of Attachment and Indiscriminate Friendliness in Children Adopted from Romanian Orphanages," *Child Development,* 69, 1092–1106.

12. Cook, T. D.; Herman, M. R.; Phillips, M. and Settersten, R. A. (2002), "Some Ways in Which Neighborhoods, Nuclear Families, Friendship Groups and Schools Jointly Affect Changes in Early Adolescent Development," *Child Development,* July 2002; Schwartz, D.; Dodge, K.; Petit, K. A.; and Bates, J. (2000), "Friendship as a Moderating Factor in the Pathway Between Early Harsh Home Environment and Later Victimization in the Peer Group," *Developmental Psychology,* 36, 646–662; Sampson, R. J.; Raudenbush, S. W.; and Earls, F. (1997), "Neighborhoods and Violent Crime: A Multilevel study of Collective Efficacy," *Science,* 277, 918–924.

13. See Froelich, J. C. (1997), "Opioid peptides," *Alcohol Health and Research World,* 21, 132–135, and Pihl, R. O. and Peterson, J. B. (1995), "Alcoholism: The Role of Different Motivational Systems," *Journal of Psychiatry and Neuroscience, 20,* 372–396.

14. See, for example, Bremner, Douglas, J.; Randall, Penny; Scott, Tammy M.; et al. (1995), "MRI-Based Measurement of Hippocampal Volume in Patients with Combat-Related Posttraumatic Stress Disorder," *American Journal of Psychiatry 152*(7): 973–981.

15. Sapolsky, R. M. (1997), "The Importance of a Well-Groomed Child," *Science* 277, 1620–1621.

16. Some work by Tiffany Field "Massage therapy effects," *American Psychologist, 53,* 1270–1281; (2002), "Massage Therapy: A Review," *Medical*

Clinics of North America, 86, 163–171; and (1999) "American Adolescents Touch Each Other Less and Are More Aggressive Toward Their Peers as Compared with French Adolescents," *Adolescence,* 34, 753–758.

17. Sources used for historical background on the Great Depression include Edsforth, R., *The New Deal: America's Response to the Great Depression,* Malden, MA: Blackwell Publishers, 2000; Klein, M., *Rainbow's End: The Crash of 1929,* Oxford, U.K.: Oxford University Press, 2001; and Turkel, S., *Hard Times: An Oral History of the Great Depression,* New York: The New Press, 1970.

18. Elder, G. H. and Conger, R. *Children of the Land: Adversity and Success in Rural America,* Chicago: University of Chicago Press, 2000.

19. Elder, G. H., Jr., *Children of the Great Depression: Social Change in Life Experience,* Chicago: University of Chicago Press, 1974; Elder, G. H. and Hareven, T. K., "Rising Above Life's Disadvantage: From the Great Depression to War," in Elder, G. H., Modell, J. and Parke, R., eds., *Children in Time and Place: Developmental and Historical Insights,* Cambridge, U.K.: Cambridge University Press, 1993, pp. 27–46.

20. Ibid.

21. LaRossa, R., *The Modernization of Fatherhood: A Social and Political History,* Chicago: University of Chicago Press, 1997.

22. Youniss, J. and Smoller, J. *Adolescent Relations with Mothers, Fathers, and Friends,* Chicago: University of Chicago Press, 1985.

23. For general sources on the salutary effects of father involvement see Parke. R. D., *Fatherhood,* Cambridge, MA: Harvard University Press 1996; and Lamb, M. E., ed., *The Role of the Father in Child Development,* New York: Wiley, 1997.

24. Cherlin, A. J.; and Furstenberg, F. F., *The New American Grandparent,* Cambridge, MA: Harvard University Press, 1992.

25. Quote from page 107 of Elder, G. H. and Conger, R., *Children of the Land: Adversity and Success in Rural America,* Chicago: University of Chicago Press, 2000.

26. *Ibid.,* p. 191.

27. See: Snyder, N. H.; and Sickmund, M., *Juvenile Offenders and Victims: 1999 National Report,* Washington, D.C.: National Center for Juvenile Justice, 1999.

CHAPTER 4
Tough Times Call for Strong Parents

1. The best source I found on the flu pandemic is Crosby, A. W., *America's Forgotten Pandemic: The Influenza of 1918,* Cambridge, U.K.: Cambridge University Press, 1989. Death rates in American cities during the epidemic are found on pages 60–61. See also Kolata, G., *Flu: The Story of the Great Influenza*

Pandemic of 1918 and the Search for the Virus That Caused It, New York: Touchstone, 1999.

2. In Boston, the first American city to experience the plague—the first wave coming at Fort Devens, an overcrowded staging area outside the city—the initial reaction was denial. See article from September 18, 1918, in the *Boston Daily Globe*: Robinson, W. J., "Devens Excited by Spanish Influenza." The *Boston Daily Globe*, Wednesday Morning, September 25, 1918, p. 1, commenting on the fort's outbreak said: "About the only persons who aren't making a fuss about the epidemic are headquarters officers and medical men. They are a little bit disgusted over the excitement that has been caused by the disease." Then, with an implicit understanding that the fittest would survive—the philosophy of Social Darwinism was quite popular at the time—the article states: "The Southern Negroes in camp have proved exceptionally susceptible to the epidemic and it is for the most part men whose constitutions are in just the proper state to absorb the disease who have any kind of a serious time."

3. Gibson, E. J. and Walk, R. D. (1960), The "Visual Cliff," *Scientific American,* 202, 67–71.

4. See, for example, Hirschberg, L. M.; and Svejda, M. (1990), "When Infants Look to Their Parents: I. Infant's Social Referencing of Mothers Compared to Fathers," *Child Development,* 61, 1175–1186; Sorce, J., Emde, R. N.; Campos, J. J.; and Klinnert, M. (1985), "Maternal Emotional Signaling: Its Effect On the Visual Cliff Behavior of 1 Year Olds," *Developmental Psychology,* 21, 195–200.

5. See, for example, Zahn-Waxler, C.; Radke-Yarrow, M.; and King, R. A. (1979), "Child Rearing and Children's Prosocial Initiations Towards Victims of Distress," *Child Development,* 50, 319–330.

6. Klinnert, M. D.; Emde, R. N.; Butterfield, P.; and Campos, J. J. (1987), "Social Referencing: The Infant's Use of Emotional Signals from a Friendly Adult with Mother Present," *Developmental Psychology,* 22, 427–432.

7. Eisenberg, N.; Fabes, R. A.; and Murphy, B. C. (1996), "Parents' Reactions to Children's Negative Emotions: Relations to Children's Social Competence and Comforting Behavior," *Child Development,* 67, 2227–2247.

8. For background information on the Blitz, I drew on information provided at the Museum of London Web site: *http://www.museum-london.org.uk/MOLsite/exhibits/blitz.* For technical information on the V1 and V2 see *http://www.accessweb.com/users/mconstab/v1.htm* and *http://www.accessweb.com/users/mconstab/v2.htm.*

9. Saluter, A. "Marital Status and Living Arrangements," March 1995 (update), *Current Population Reports,* Washington, D.C.: U.S. Department of Commerce, Census Bureau, 1996, pp. 20–191. Available at *http://www.census.-gov/prod/2/pop/p20/p20-491.pdf.*

10. An excellent summary of research on children's reactions to divorce

ENDNOTES

can be found in Hetherington, E. M.: Bridges, M.; and Insabella, G. M. (1998), "What Matters? What Does Not? Five Perspectives on the Association Between Marital Transitions and Children's Adjustment," *American Psychologist,* 53, 167–184.

11. Rutter, M. (1996) "Stress Research: Accomplishments and Tasks Ahead," in Haggerty, R. J.; Sherrod, L. R.; Garmezy, N. and Rutter, M., (eds.) *Stress, Risk, and Resilience in Children and Adolescents: Processes, Mechanisms, and Interventions,* Cambridge, U.K.: Cambridge University Press, 1996, pp. 354–386; and Clark, D.; Pynoos, R. S. and Goebel, A. E., "Mechanisms and Processes of Adolescent Bereavement," in ibid., pp. 100–146.

12. Rutter, M. (1996), "Stress Research: Accomplishments and Tasks Ahead," in ibid., pp. 354–386.

13. Sources for Colombian history are Betancourt, I., *Until Death Do Us Part: My Struggles to Reclaim Colombia,* New York: HarperCollins, 2002; Rohter, L. (2000), "Cocaine War: A Special Report; a Web of Drugs and Strife in Colombia," *New York Times,* April 21, 2000; Forero, J. (2002), "Administration Shifts Focus on Colombia aid," *New York Times,* February 6, 2002; and Bowden, M., *Killing Pablo,* London: Penguin, 2001.

CHAPTER 5
The Big Picture

1. Schuster, Mark A. et al. (2001), "National Survey of Stress Reactions After the September 11, 2001, Terrorist Attacks," *New England Journal of Medicine* 345, 1507–1512.

2. McIntosh, D. N.; Cohen Silver, R.; and Wortman, C. B. (1993), "Religion's Role in Adjustment to a Negative Life Event: Coping with the Loss of a Child," *Journal of Consulting and Clinical Psychology* 65, 812–821.

3. A Harris Poll in August 2000 found that among a representative sample of Americans over age seventeen, 93.8 percent said that they believed in God, 88.8 percent believed in heaven, and 73 percent believed in hell. In contrast, only 41 percent of poll respondents believed in astrology. The figures for belief in God appear to be holding fairly steady during the years spanning the Millennial generation. A 1986 *USA Today* poll of a representative sample of Americans eighteen and older found that 95.5 percent believed in God or a supreme being (poll results available at: *http://cgi.irss.unc.edu/tempdocs/14:58:36:90.htm*).

4. Robert Putnam reports on trends in church and synagogue attendance in Chapter 4 of his book *Bowling Alone: The Collapse and Revival of American Community,* New York: Simon and Schuster, 2000. Roughly speaking, weekly attendance at religious services peaked in the late 1950s at around 47 percent of Americans. By 2000, this figure was approximately 37 percent. Interestingly, Putnam believes that these figures represent an *over-report*. That is, people often remember (or report) going to religious services when in reality, they have not. In my Parenting Practices at the Millennium Survey of 1,060 middle- and upper-class parents of children ages four through eighteen, 48 percent reported never or hardly ever attending religious services, 17.2 percent said they went about once per month, and 34.8 percent reported going once per week or more. Sandra Hofferth reports on her research conducted at the University of Michigan over the course of sixteen years beginning in 1981. Children's free time has declined 16 percent over this period (from 63 hours per week to 51 hours per week) and time not spent in school or doing regular activities such as eating and sleeping is more structured. Churchgoing declined 40 percent during this period. See Hofferth, S. L., (1999), "Changes in Children's Time 1981–1997," *Center Survey 9*, no. 1.

5. See Jones, S. L. (1994), "A Constructive Relationship for Religion with the Science and Profession of Psychology: Perhaps the Boldest Move Yet," *American Psychologist, 6*, 184–199.

6. The most exhaustive study of religion and coping that I found is Pargament, K. I., *The Psychology of Religion and Coping: Theory, Research, and Practice*, New York: Guilford Press, 1997. Three other useful sources were Tix, A. P.; and Frazier, P. A. (1998), "The Use of Religious Coping During Stressful Life Events: Main Effects, Moderation, and Mediation," *Journal of Consulting and Clinical Psychology*, 66, 411–422; McIntosh, D. N.; Cohen Silver, R.; and Wortman, C. B. (1993), "Religion's Role in Adjustment to a Negative Life Event: Coping with the Loss of a Child," *Journal of Consulting and Clinical Psychology* 65, 812–821, and Park, C.; Chen, L. H.; and Herb, L. (1990), "Intrinsic Religiousness and Religious Coping as Life Stress Moderators for Catholics versus Protestants," *Journal of Personality and Social Psychology*, 59, 562–574.

7. Mercer, D.; Lorden, R.; and Falkenberg, S. (1995), "Mediating Effects of Religiousness on the Recovery from Victimization." Paper presented at the meeting of the American Psychological Association, New York. Reported in Pargament, *The Psychology of Religion and Coping*, New York: Guilford, 1997.

8. See Brody, G.; Stoneman, Z.; and Flor, D. (1996), "Parental Religiosity, Family Processes, and Youth Competence in Rural, Two-Parent African American Families," *Developmental Psychology* 32, 696–706.

9. Gazzaniga, M. S., *The Social Brain: Discovering the Networks of the Mind*, New York: Basic Books, 1985.

10. See Cantor, N. F., *In The Wake of the Plague: The Black Death and the World It Made*, New York: The Free Press, 2001; and Herlihy, D., *The Black Death*, Cambridge, MA: Harvard University Press, 1997.

11. Freud, S., *The Future of an Illusion*, Garden City, NY: Doubleday Anchor, 1927–1964.

12. For a list see *http://www.catholic-forum.com/saints/saintj11.htm*.

13. Frank, J. D. and Frank, J. B., *Persuasion and Healing*, Third Edition, Baltimore: Johns Hopkins University Press, 1993.

14. Shapiro, A. K. and Shapiro, E., "The Placebo: Is It Much Ado About Nothing?" in Harrington, A. (ed.), *The Placebo Effect*, Cambridge, MA: Harvard University Press, 1997, pp. 12–36.

15. *Ibid.*

16. Alexander, K. L. and Entwisle, D. R. (1988), "Achievement in the First Two Years of School: Patterns and Processes," *Monographs of the Society for Research in Child Development*, Serial no. 218, v. 53, no. 2.

17. Rabiner, D.; and Coie, J. (1989), "Effects of Expectancy Inductions on Children's Acceptance by Unfamiliar Peers," *Developmental Psychology*, 25, 450–457.

18. A classic book on person's experiences of religion is James, William (1904), *The Varieties of Religious Experience*, London: Penguin, 1985. See also Capps, D.; and Capps, W. H., *The Religious Personality*, Belmont, CA: Wadsworth, 1970.

19. Quote is the conclusion to the essay "The World as I See It," which is taken from the abridged edition of Einstein's book bearing the same title. In the abridged edition (New York: Philosophical Library, 1949), the essay appears on pp. 1–5.

20. A full listing of Alcoholics Anonymous's Twelve Steps can be found at *http://www.alcoholics-anonymous.org/english/E_FactFile/M-24_d6.html.*

21. See Ambrose, Stephen E., *The Wild Blue: The Men and Boys Who Flew the B-24's over Germany*, New York: Simon and Schuster, 2001.

22. See, for example, Seligman, M. E. P. (1990), *Learned Optimism*, New York: Simon and Schuster, 1990; and Seligman, M. E., *The Optimistic Child*, New York: Harper, 1995.

23. Irish history sources include Fields, R. M., *Society Under Siege: A Psychology of Northern Ireland*, Philadelphia: Temple University Press, 1976; Foster, R. F., *The Oxford Illustrated History of Ireland*, Oxford U.K.: Oxford University Press, 1978; and two Web-based sources: *www.iol.ie/~dluby/history. htm* and *www.vms.utexas.edu/~jdana/history/chronology.html.* For information on incidents at the Holy Cross school see, for example, Unsworth, M. (2002) "Holy Cross Suffers Drop in Pupils," *Irish Times*, March 2, 2002. and *www. ryans.org/childrenofireland/Index.htm.*

24. Theresa told me that she had gone there as a consultant to the Children Affected by Armed Conflict Unit at the International Rescue Committee—a non-governmental organization based in New York City.

25. Quote is from page 233 of Moskovitz, S., *Love Despite Hate: Child Survivors of the Holocaust and Their Adult Lives*, New York: Schocken Books, 1983.

26. See comprehensive review in Pargament, K. I., *The Psychology of Reli-*

gion and Coping: Theory, Research, and Practice, New York: Guilford Press, 1997.

CHAPTER 6
Moving On

1. The most cogent writing on the subject of memory and trauma is by Besel A. Van der Kolk. The primary sources for this section include an edited volume: van der Kolk, B. A.; McFarlane, A. C.; and Weisaeth, L. D., eds., *Traumatic Stress: The Effects of Overwhelming Experience on Mind, Body, and Society*, New York: The Guilford Press and single works: van der Kolk, B. A. (1994), "The Body Keeps the Score: Memory and the Evolving Psychobiology of Post-traumatic Stress," *Harvard Review of Psychiatry,* 1: 253–65; van der Kolk, B. A.; Pelcovitz, D.; Roth, S., et al. (1996), "Dissociation, somatization, and affect dysregulation: the complexity of adaptation of trauma." *American Journal of Psychiatry,* 153 (Supplement), 83–93.

2. This case is discussed in depth in: van der Kolk, B. A., *Psychological Trauma*, Washington, D.C: American Psychiatry Press, 1987.

3. See: Ross Buck: *Human Motivation and Emotion*, Chapter 4, New York: Wiley and Sons, 1988.

4. Van der Kolk, B.A., "Trauma and Memory," in Van der Kolk, B. A.; McFarlane, A. C.; and Weisaeth, L., eds. *Traumatic Stress: The Effects of Overwhelming Experience on Mind, Body, and Society*, New York: The Guilford Press, pp. 279–302.

5. *Ibid.*

6. Wise, R. A. (1988), "The neurobiology of craving: Implications for the understanding and treatment of addiction," *Journal of Abnormal Psychology,* 97, 118–132.

7. See Kindlon, D.; Mezzacappa, E.; and Earls, F. (1995), "Psychometric Properties of Impulsivity Measures: Temporal Stability, Validity, and Factor Structure," *Journal of Child Psychology and Psychiatry and Allied Disciplines*, 645–661; and Kindlon, D. J.; Tremblay, R. E.; Mezzacappa, E.; Earls, F.; Laurent, D.; and Schaal, B. (1995), "Longitudinal Patterns of Heart Rate and Fighting Behavior in 9- through 12-Year-Old Boys," *Journal of the American Academy of Child and Adolescent Psychiatry,* 34, 371–377.

8. Sources for this section include: Rothbaum, B. O.; and Foa, E. B. (1996), "Cognitive-Behavioral Therapy for Post-traumatic Stress Disorder," in Van der Kolk, B. A.; McFarlane, A. C. and L. Weisaeth, eds., *Traumatic Stress: The Effects of Overwhelming Experience on Mind, Body, and Society*, New York: The Guilford Press, 1996, pp. 491–509; Layne, C. M. et al. (2001), "Trauma/Grief-Focused Group Psychotherapy School-Based Postwar Intervention with Traumatized Bosnian Adolescents," *Group Dynamics: Theory, Research and*

Practice, 5, 277–290; and Stubendort, K.; Donnelly, G. R.; and Cohen, J. A. (2001), "Cognitive-Behavioral Therapy for Bereaved Adults and Children Following an Air Disaster," *Group Dynamics: Theory, Research, and Practice,* 5, 261–276.

9. See: Martin, Rod A. (2001), "Humor, Laughter, and Physical Health: Methodological Issues and Research Findings," *Psychological Bulletin,* 127(4): 504–519.

CHAPTER 7
Grace Under Pressure

1. Baumeister, R. F. and Leary, M. R. (1995) "The need to belong: Desire for interpersonal attachments as a fundamental human motivation," *Psychological Bulletin,* 117, 497–529.

2. An excellent review of research on stress and coping in children and adolescents may be found in Compas, Bruce E.; Connor-Smith, Jennifer K.; Saltzman, Heidi; Thomsen, Alexandra Harding; and Wadsworth, Martha E. (2001), "Coping With Stress During Childhood and Adolescence: Problems, Progress, and Potential in Theory and Research," *Psychological Bulletin* 227(1): 87–127.

3. Seligman, M. E., *The Optimistic Child,* New York: Harper, 1995.

4. Freud, A.; and Burlingham, D. T., *War and Children,* New York: International University Press, 1994.

5. Weisenberg, M.; Schwarzwald, J.; Waysman, M.; Solomon, Z.; and Klingman, A. (1993), "Coping of School-Age Children in the Sealed Room During SCUD Missile Bombardment and Postwar Stress Reactions," *Journal of Consulting and Clinical Psychology,* 61, 462–467.

6. See: Compas, Bruce E.; Connor-Smith, Jennifer K.; Saltzman, Heidi; Thomsen, Alexandra Harding; and Wadsworth, Martha E. (2001), "Coping With Stress During Childhood and Adolescence: Problems, Progress, and Potential in Theory and Research," *Psychological Bulletin* 227(1): 87–127.

7. Frankl, V. E., *Man's Search for Meaning,* New York: Pocket Books, 1984.

ACKNOWLEDGMENTS

My greatest joy in writing this book was having the opportunity to get to know the remarkable people who inhabit its pages. Thank you, Steve Ross, Prudence Paine, Marion Haas, Sean McManus, Jothy Rosenberg, Jane Brown, Mary Beth Tipton, Theresa Stichick, and George McGovern for giving me your time and sharing your past. You (and your remarkable parents) have been, each in your own way, an inspiration to me. I hope that I have been able to adequately transfer the gifts you gave me to the people who will read this book.

My deep gratitude also goes to the many other people I interviewed whose names do not appear in this book, each of them with remarkable stories to tell. I especially wanted to thank Millie Von Tulin, Callie Fay Baker, Abraham Gutman, Diana Gomez, and Mike and Norma Stichick. Millie, who died only a few months after our interview, deserves special mention. The afternoon I spent with this remarkable one-hundred-year old music teacher listening to her celebrate her life (and sing songs from the Civil War that she had heard at her grandfather's knee) was an unforgettable joy.

I want to thank Joe and Bess Kindlon, my parents, for discussing their experience of America in the twentieth century, for sharing their personal stories with me, and for being resilient in the face of adversity.

Special thanks go to my personal editor, Ken Wapner, for his good company and invaluable assistance in all aspects of this enterprise. Adam Kraus, a brilliant student intern/research assistant, helped with interviews, transcriptions, and many other aspects of this production. His work was exemplary and greatly appreciated. Gail Ross, agent *extraordinaire*, was—as she has been since I have known her—a guiding light, supportive friend, and wise counsel.

I am thankful to the wonderful people at Miramax Books, especially Jonathan Burnham, Hilary Bass, and JillEllyn Riley. Jonathan's solid presence at the helm during the turbulence of post 9/11 New York was a great reassurance. Hilary, the Wonder Woman of the publicity department, was a joy to work with. I could not have asked for a finer hands-on collaborator from day one than my editor, JillEllyn. Her perspicacity, warmth, humor, support, and editorial acumen, have left their trace on each page of this book.

Finally, I am most grateful for my family's patience, support, and understanding. Julia thoughtfully discussed her reactions to tough times with me. Diana helped with transcriptions and occasionally gave me access to my computer. My wife, Catalina, not only shares her life experiences in these pages but also her deep professional understanding of the etiology and treatment of psychological trauma. My gratitude to her is boundless.